The 13TH *Disciple*

PAUL STUTZMAN

OTHER BOOKS BY PAUL STUTZMAN

The Wandering Home Series
Book One: The Wanderers
Book Two: Wandering Home
Book Three: Wander No More

Adventure Memoir
Hiking Through
   One Man's Journey to Peace and Freedom on the Appalachian Trail
Biking Across America
   My Coast-to-Coast Adventure and the People I Met Along the Way
Stuck in the Weeds
   A Pilgrim on the Mississippi River and the Camino de Santiago

With Author Serena Miller
More Than Happy: The Wisdom of Amish Parenting

CONTACT
www.paulstutzman.com
www.hikingthrough.com
www.facebook.com/pvstutzman
pstutzman@roadrunner.com

The 13TH *Disciple*

PAUL STUTZMAN

Wandering Home Books
Berlin, Ohio

Cover Art by | *Igor V. Babailov*
Design by | *Lori Troyer*

Carlisle Printing
OF WALNUT CREEK LTD
800.927.4196 · carlisleprinting.com
Sugarcreek, Ohio 44681

Dedicated to

Andrew D. Stutzman, Fred Hostetler,
Abraham Mast, Aden R. Miller, and Atlee Barkman

In my writing, I occasionally refer to my childhood church teachings in a manner that some could construe as being critical.

And yes, I did sometimes chafe a bit at some of the rules laid out by the church leadership.

However, my memories of church taken as a whole are pleasant. During my formative years and up until I was married at age 23, I was ministered to by these five men who were seeking to preach what they believed was best to prepare our souls for eternity.

All five of these church leaders had come out of an Amish background and did not have the benefit of any seminary training. The knowledge they acquired they achieved by searching the Scriptures and seeking to do God's will.

It is with deep reverence that I dedicate this book to these five men.

Their love for God instilled in me a desire to discover for myself the meaning of following Jesus.

With gratitude

If left to my own volition, the thoughts and lessons realized during my many adventures would likely never see the light of day. For a certainty, many words would possibly be written to entertain my grandchildren in some distant future—but they would never be published.

The fact that these ideas and ramblings are actually in your hand now requires a standing round of applause and a tip of my hat to several special people.

Thank you to Craig Clapper for being my guide and hiking partner during our sojourn in Israel. I couldn't find any tour groups offering hitchhiking opportunities to the Golan Heights, so I contacted Craig, who was a seasoned hiker as well as a retired minister of the Gospel. Craig had already been to Israel with several tour groups and had a reasonable sense of the lay of the land. Yes, there were times we had no idea where we were, but we were never truly lost.

Thank you to Debbie Lassiter for reaching out and introducing me to her neighbor, the accomplished portrait artist Igor V. Babailov.

Thank you to Igor and Mary Babailov for welcoming me, joining in this project, and generously bringing Igor's talent to this book.

Thank you to Elaine Starner for providing the impetus that gets my books published. This is the ninth book on which we have collaborated. Her encouragement, editing, cajoling, and interchange of ideas assures that more than my grandchildren will read my writings.

About the cover

Can you imagine living during the Golden Age of Dutch art? This was the era during which Rembrandt, Vermeer, Bosch, and other master artists produced some of the most famous art in existence.

What fascinates me about these works of art is the detail the artists have included. A person can be mesmerized by small, intricate touches in a painting of a familiar story. Rembrandt, for example, painted many scenes depicting Bible stories, like *The Storm on The Sea of Galilee* and *The Raising of Lazarus.* One of his most famous works is *The Return of the Prodigal Son,* displayed in The Hermitage Museum in St. Petersburg, Russia.

Can you also imagine being invited into the painters' homes or studios? What would it have been like to join the artist as he walked among his paintings, explaining the inspiration that put thought, genius, and paint to canvas? Although it's not possible to become a time traveler and go back to visit those painters, their work still inspires millions to this day.

I recently had the privilege of visiting with a modern-day master portrait artist.

A friend of mine informed me that her neighbor was the world-famous portrait artist Igor V. Babailov. She certainly had my immediate attention. I wanted to meet him, if that could be arranged. It was, and I found myself in the home of Igor and Mary Babailov in Brentwood, Tennessee.

The 13ᵗʰ Disciple

Igor's paintings hang in several Presidential libraries and in numerous museums around the world. He was commissioned to do portraits of the last three popes, and these portraits are exhibited in the Vatican. He has taught at the Florence Academy of Art in Italy and lectures at universities and art venues around the world. His numerous awards include being elected as an Honorary American Academician of the Russian Academy of Arts.

One can only imagine the honor and reverence I felt as Igor took me through his studio, showing me many of his beautiful works.

Later, sitting in the Babailovs' living room, I entertained them with stories of my recent trip to Israel. I told about sitting by the Sea of Galilee and wondering what it would have been like to be there when Jesus picked His disciples. I spoke about being on the hillside where Jesus fed the 5,000. There He took several loaves of bread and miraculously multiplied them to have enough food to feed the entire crowd. I noted a detail that had recently been impressed upon me: Jesus did not distribute the bread. He gave it to His disciples to serve the crowd. I described my visit to the site of the last supper, where Jesus did offer the bread and cup to His disciples. In essence, what Jesus was doing at the last supper was akin to the feeding of the 5,000. He gave his body as living bread to His disciples with the intention that they would feed the crowds living bread following His death.

I voiced my desire to create a book cover that could make folks curious about who The 13th Disciple might be. Yes, the possibility of having Igor Babailov create a painting for the book excited me, but I also realized I didn't have the resources required to hire a master painter.

I shouldn't have been concerned about that, since I serve a Master who can do the impossible.

A gift of inspiration came then. Mary Babailov suggested a scene where Jesus offers His body and blood to an enquiring pilgrim. The rest of us in the room knew, with a clarity from the Spirit, that this was exactly what the cover should portray.

Igor sat back in his chair and was silent for a short period of time.

After a while, he exclaimed, "I've got it, and I'll do it!"

An image had formed in his mind, and now that image is the art you see on this book cover.

Look at it, question it. Art speaks every language known to man. What does it speak to you?

My prayer is that you will contemplate the scene and place yourself at the feet of Jesus. Ask to be His disciple, then silently listen to what Jesus might be saying to you.

For more information on Igor V. Babailov and to view many of his masterpieces, go to www.babailov.homestead.com.

Table of Contents

Introduction

Up until a year ago, I had never felt an inclination to visit what we call "the Holy Land." It just wasn't on my radar. Then the opportunity arose, an invitation was extended, and I simply knew that I must pursue plans to make this hike happen. I *knew*. It was a clear call that I was compelled to follow.

If you haven't followed my wanderings and wonderings before, here's a quick background:

I was raised on church rules. That's what formed my thinking and shaped my behavior. It's likely I was already absorbing church rules while still in the womb.

That's also why, in 1969, during the waning weeks of the Vietnam War, I turned eighteen and registered with the draft board as a conscientious objector. Born Amish and raised in a strict Mennonite church, I never even considered military service because killing others, even those who were trying to kill us, was against one of our church's most distinctive and strongly held beliefs.

After graduating from high school (which was, by the way, not exactly a breaking of church rules, but at least a break with our tradition), I had no desire to follow the expected route that most of our young men took into a life of carpentry or masonry. I chose, instead, to volunteer two years of alternate service at a hospital in a neighboring city.

In that environment, I ran headlong into the world beyond the sheltered, relatively carefree place in which I had spent my early years. My interactions with the doctors, nurses, and patients opened a window through which I glimpsed lives quite different than the one I knew. Values and lifestyles were far removed from my own. Incidents and details that many of you might consider slight and insignificant jolted my comfortable thinking. Televisions were constantly playing (strictly forbidden in our church); I heard words I'd never encountered before (beyond hospital terminology!); and smoking was an accepted, commonplace habit (a sin against the temple of God, I'd been taught).

We all have one thing in common, though—death. Life and death met at that hospital, and I was a witness and a student. In my first-day tour of the facility, we passed one room where staff were using a defibrillator to resuscitate a man. The paddles were in place, I heard the "Clear!" and the body lurched above the bed. As I cared for and learned to know patients, I heard stories from army veterans and old folks who were fading away. Looking into the face of death changes one's perspective on many things. I listened to the stories of folks who knew they were approaching death or who had felt its shadow cross their path through illness or surgery, and I learned a great deal.

Every morning, my shift started with "report." My co-workers and I would meet with the lead nurse from the night shift, who would report on the night's activities. *Mr. So-and-So was admitted for congestive heart failure. The patient in 101 expired during the night. Apparently not enough change in his parking meter.*

At the end of report, I was handed a sheet with my assignments for the day. Some days the workload was staggering; other days, I found it very manageable. My tasks included feeding and bathing patients who could not manage these challenges on their own. I also changed bed linens—quite an ordeal if the patient is bedfast. (You roll the patient to one side, then remove dirty linens and insert clean linens simultaneously. Push, shove, and roll the patient the other direction, and you're halfway done.)

Thus, one word always caught my attention when I glanced at my assignments for the day. I rejoiced at seeing the word *ambulatory*, as I would rejoice in welcoming a good, helpful friend.

Ambulatory patients were allowed to get out of bed and walk. *Hallelujah, off to the shower you go whilst I make your bed.* Other patients required time- and energy-consuming attention, but the duties I performed for ambulatory patients were quickly dispatched.

The most enjoyable of those duties was to ambulate patients who were ambulatory. That simply meant taking Mr. Smith by the elbow and walking down the promenade with him. I liked that because I liked ambulating myself. While the patient and I ambulated, I also heard interesting stories about life, liberty, and the pursuit of happiness. As I walked alongside older folks in the waning years of their lives, I often heard reflections on how precious life itself was. In addition, I became aware of how much I was learning just by the simple movement of my body. You can't be dead while still moving, so keep moving.

From that beginning, ambulating has become a beneficial and necessary thing in my life.

Following my wife's death, I determined to put ambulation to the utmost test. I decided to hike the entire 2,176-mile Appalachian Trail (AT), hoping that such an extended time walking through nature would help me work out what my life would be after that great loss. The grueling trek took me through three hundred deep valleys and over three hundred mountain tops, and it did bring incredible healing and insights into my life.

That hike also changed my relationship with God, but I still had questions for Him. Even before my wife's death, I had struggled to understand what it meant to be a Christian, a follower of Jesus. What should the Christian life look like and be? What did it mean to believe in Jesus? If I claimed to follow Jesus Christ, how would that shape my life? My questioning was probably intensified because … well, after all … I was into the second half-century of my life and *shouldn't I know this by now?*

In the years following the AT hike, I continued to ask these questions. One search for answers took me to Spain, where I was determined to ambulate across the country on the Camino de Santiago, a pilgrimage trail. That hike is also known as the Way of Saint James. James was one of Jesus' twelve disciples, and when Jesus said to "go into all the world," James went to what was then thought to be the end of the earth—Spain. Today, he is the patron saint of Spain, and everywhere in the towns and along the trail, I saw statues and images of this disciple. I tried to imagine what James had witnessed as one of Jesus' close friends, what he'd felt, and how it had compelled him to "follow" Jesus as a wandering missionary for the rest of his life. Several incidents during that hike convinced me that I was edging closer to the truth of what it means to follow Jesus.

Following each of these hikes, I returned home and wrote a book about the experience. Besides creating vicarious adventures for my readers, the books were also my attempts to sort out new insights and partial answers that God had given me while I was ambulating along the trails.

However, in spite of all I'd learned on the Appalachian Trail and the Camino de Santiago, I was still reading the Scriptures with a measure of perplexity. I'm well aware of Jesus' words that one has to accept Him and have faith in Him just as a child would accept and trust. But I found that difficult. Too many questions kept stomping around in my head.

Following Jesus is supposedly the most important choice for a person to make. Heaven and hell lie in the balance. So why is it so confusing, even difficult, to comprehend some of the things Jesus said and did? That was one line of my questioning. I had always believed all those stories about Jesus because I believed what my parents told me. I believed "about" Jesus because that's what my church teachers and leaders taught me from youth to adulthood. I had declared my allegiance to Jesus; I wanted to follow Him. Yet I knew there was something still missing in my reading of and understanding of the Scriptures.

I look back over those years and experiences to explain the call to Israel in 2016. Yes, I truly believe it was a call. Just as surely as Jesus walked along the Sea of Galilee and called out to fishermen to join Him or as He walked through a town and stopped at a tax collector's booth to extend the same invitation, so He has been leading me down a path, always inviting me to follow Him a little more closely and with clearer sight. That's why I've had the audacity to choose the title you see on the front of this book.

The trail that beckoned me is called the Jesus Trail.

What better way to bring understanding to my wondering mind than to go walk where Jesus walked, to actually ambulate in the footsteps of Jesus, to "follow" Him through His years as a human being on this earth and to learn from Him. I had never dreamed I would do this; but unexpectedly, I was convinced I *must* do it.

I know that many folks who were born into and reared on the Gospel, in insular communities like my own, still find it difficult to grasp the true meaning of believing in Jesus and following Him. One day in Israel, I was explaining my perplexity at this paradox to my hiking partner, Craig.

"It's simple," said he. "You were born and raised in a barn."

Say what?

He went on to explain, and his analysis made sense.

Jesus was born in a manger, and I was born in a barn.

And therein lay the obstruction.

CHAPTER 1

From Touchdown Jesus to Jesus' Touchdown

A former Marine and a conscientious objector were strolling the campus of Notre Dame University.

That sounds like the beginning of a good joke, doesn't it?

Except that it wasn't a joke. It was my real life, and I was on a quest. I was just outside of South Bend, Indiana. Later that afternoon, Craig, my hiking partner, and I would be flying out of Chicago, headed to Israel. That morning, Craig noted that we had several hours to spend ambulating somewhere, and he gave me two options: a local park or the campus of Notre Dame University.

I didn't hesitate. Without question, it would be Notre Dame, home of the Fighting Irish. I am a college football fan. I'm also from Amish Country. The two might not seem to have any connection, but there's a common play on words that gave rise to a mythical "Yoder Dame, home of the Fighting Amish." You can even buy

T-shirts bearing the words and logos.

However, it wasn't the football stadium that I most wanted to see. I was seeking Touchdown Jesus.

The official name of this large mosaic mural is "The Word of Life." On the wall of Notre Dame's Hesburgh Library, 134 feet high and 68 feet wide, the mural depicts saints and scholars from many eras; and standing above them all, with arms upraised, is the resurrected Jesus, the Source of all words of life, wisdom, and truth.

The mosaic on the library wall is adjacent to the football stadium and used to be easily visible to the television audience as they followed the Fighting Irish football games. Jesus' upraised arms resemble a referee signaling a touchdown, and although additions to the stadium have obscured the wall somewhat, the mural is still nicknamed "Touchdown Jesus."

"So where is this library with Touchdown Jesus?" I asked, as we strolled along.

Craig, the ex-Marine of our opening line, is a minister of the Gospel, and he was too busy explaining the intricacies of hiring pastors to hear my question. He had recently retired, and on our way to Notre Dame, we had driven by the church that he had pastored. Over twenty-seven years' time, he had shepherded a flock that grew from several families into a thriving congregation. Our conversation had been about the many ways in which pastoring (his former job) and restaurant managing (my former job) were similar. One of those similar areas was the task of hiring employees.

On the university campus, my mind had moved on to Touchdown Jesus, but Craig was still talking about the interviewing process for pastoral applicants. One red flag, he noted, was when an applicant arrived for an interview and wasn't carrying a Bible. That detail in itself was enough to eliminate the person from the list of candidates.

Craig told of some folks who had joined his congregation only after spending a considerable amount of time looking for a suitable church. They wanted a strong, Bible-believing church. So they would park in church parking lots, observing people as they arrived for a service. If folks weren't carrying Bibles, the prospective members fled the scene to stake out another congregation from the parking lot. They finally found their new church home with Craig's flock. This was a church of Bible carriers, but I silently observed that this must have taken place before iPhones and apps with thirty versions of the sacred writ were the "Bibles" folks carry to church.

My attention to Craig's discourse on church polices and hiring practices was interrupted by the scene unfolding before us. Students crisscrossed the campus, going hither and yon to various chambers of higher learning. And there, rising above a cluster of trees, was the wall portraying the likeness of Jesus with outstretched arms.

I took a look, and that was enough for me. *Okay, I've been here, I've seen it. Let's go to Israel.*

We did, however, continue to tour the campus, strolling around the lake and visiting the log chapel where the mission and school first started.

By this time, Craig was talking about conversations he'd had with retired pastors, asking what they would do differently if they could relive their years of ministry. One man said he would rely more on volunteer help instead of paid personnel. I wondered if I could have run restaurants with volunteer help.

Another pastor said he would have hired more judiciously and fired more quickly. "You must get rid of those church cancers sooner rather than later. They can destroy a church." Cancer can invade any troop of employees, whether in church or restaurant or factory. I knew firsthand how deadly it can be.

The world itself was invaded by a sinister cancer many years ago, and the cancer exists to this day. The antidote was delivered as a baby, born to grow up and take that cancer upon Himself so that others could be healed.

I was eager to go to Bethlehem, to see where Touchdown Jesus had actually touched down.

. . .

Recently, I was the speaker at an Amish Christmas event. I spoke about my trip to Israel and how it had changed the way I now read my Bible.

In a conversation that evening, an Amish man told me that he would love to visit the Holy Land, but flying was prohibited. Church rules, you know. Yes, I certainly knew about church rules; I was raised on them myself. Early in my youth, I thought I'd figured out the guiding principle behind church rules: If anything was fun or exciting, it was probably forbidden. At least, that was the perception that evolved in my teenage mind.

So I asked the Amish man longing for travel, "Do your church leaders know how miserable it is to fly? Are they perhaps under some misunderstanding that it's an enjoyable experience?"

To fly from Chicago to Tel Aviv, Israel, is to spend fifteen hours confined in a tight, metal soup can, breathing air already used by over four hundred other inhabitants. In addition, our flight was blessed with a screaming baby, who apparently had opinions similar to mine on the wonders and pleasures of flying.

In Paris, France, we needed to switch planes and change to the Israeli airline of El Al. This airline is notorious for tight security and thorough examinations of weary, all-night travelers. Our interrogation didn't quite reach the level of waterboarding, but the two Israeli security guards sure knew their stuff.

The two guards were young women. In Israel, most young people are required to join the military. Men serve three years; women, two years. A certain group of Orthodox Jews is exempt from military service. These are called *Haredi* Jews, the strictest and most removed from modern culture. Reading the Torah and applying it to every detail of their lives seems to be their one focus.

During our time in Israel, we had conversations with Israeli soldiers who referred to *haredim* (Haredi Jews) as *prayer soldiers.* For obvious reasons, they were not highly regarded by most military personnel. In the United States, a parallel might be the tension between soldiers and conscientious objectors.

My weary fellow sojourner and I were separated for individual interrogations. Craig convinced the young security guard that he wasn't a spy or any other sort of nefarious character and was set free. Then the guard turned her attention to me.

I will admit (and you already know I'm far from politically correct), my first impression was that this young lady was altogether too attractive to be working security. She should have been on television, reading the news or explaining the weather or modeling clothes for some upscale company.

Her good looks, though, were offset by a stone coldness in her eyes. I quickly realized that I'd better not try any of my humorous banter on her. She undoubtedly could have dismantled me, limb from limb, in one blink of those black eyes.

"What is your reason for going to Israel?" she asked.

"I'm going to the Holy Land to hike the Jesus Trail."

She had never heard of that trail until recently—as recently as five minutes ago, apparently. I had overheard Craig explain to her the nature of our quest. Craig had also told her that he was a retired minister and was going to guide me around Israel. She could not comprehend what *minister* meant until he explained that it was similar to a Christian *rabbi*. It seemed she was still trying to absorb the meaning of that when she interrogated me.

She perused my passport and then looked up, scrutinizing me.

"You're Jewish, aren't you?" I'm convinced the makings of a smile appeared with this question.

"Who, me? No, I'm not Jewish."

"You have Jewish features."

"I do?" I asked, astounded.

Then I realized the clue that she had picked up. Many Jewish names end in -*man*. Look at a list of Jewish people, and you'll see names such as Goldman, Lieberman, Bronfman, Silverman, and Neumann. The name on my passport was *Stutzman*. My mind jumped to my family tree—my paternal grandmother was *Kaufman*. *Hallelujah, I'm Jewish! I'm included with God's chosen people.*

I kept those thoughts to myself, though. Those black eyes were still all business.

It was doubtful that I was Jewish. But I know I'm still chosen!

. . .

In the Paris airport, Craig called my attention to a scene unfolding directly across the concourse.

"Look," Craig said. "He's showing off."

I'm always fascinated by these little vignettes of life. This one was straight out of the Bible, a scene from Matthew, chapter 23.

That's the chapter with the "seven woes." Jesus was dressing down the Pharisees and the teachers of the law, accusing them of tying heavy loads upon folks' shoulders and doing nothing to actually help them move. Jesus also denounced their showboating. "You just want people to see you," He said. These hypocrites wore garments bedecked with long tassels down the sides, and they wore phylacteries large enough for all to see.

Unless you are employed at a phylactery factory, you may not know exactly what that is. A phylactery is a small black box, often leather, containing an assortment of Old Testament verses. During prayers, one is attached to the forehead with a band, and the other is attached to the left forearm. It's meant to be a reminder of the words of God.

Jesus was reprimanding those who would sit at prominent places, with their tassels and phylacteries chosen and arranged to attract attention. These religious folks reveled in being seen and acknowledged as rabbis. Jesus, however, was not impressed; and in Matthew 23, He dissects their bad intentions with laser precision.

In a far corner of the concourse of the Paris terminal, a Jewish man was going through the rituals of prayer.

Jews have a duty to pray three times a day, and these prayers normally last up to one half hour. The morning prayer is called *shacharit*. It's a prayer akin to climbing a ladder upward to God. The first few rungs of the ladder are verses of praise, followed by acknowledging the awesome accomplishments of God. Eventually you reach the top rung of the ladder and approach God, making your requests known. Then back toward terra firma you go, with prayers of penitence as you descend from the heavenly realms, back to deal with your earthly day.

I realize that's merely scratching the surface of what prayer means to a Jewish person. But if we're going to talk of scratching the surface, consider the time that Jews spend in prayer. I did the math.

The 13th Disciple

Three times a day at thirty minutes each—that's about an hour and twenty-five minutes longer than many Christians. How many of us barely even scratch the surface when it comes to dialogue with God?

This fellow in the corner of the terminal—who, by the way, was the father of the crying child who had serenaded us all the way across the pond—had found a semi-secluded area to have his morning prayers. But as we watched, it was obvious his rituals were not preparing him to pray, but preparing a show. In full view of everyone, he strapped on the phylacteries, making them "wide, and his tassels long."

I was divided in my opinion of this public prayer warrior. On one hand, he wanted to be seen. On the other hand, he had the courage to be seen. How many of us grafted-in Christians are hesitant to be seen bowing our heads for a short prayer in a public place? And when we "strap on our phylacteries" and hear Scripture read, does it flow over our ears like water over hard ground? Or do the words of God penetrate and revive us?

If I was possibly Jewish, I wondered if I should give some consideration to shopping for phylacteries. I did, eventually. They were over $200, and I decided to pass, for the time being.

. . .

I don't pretend to know why, but many Jewish people seem to be smarter than the rest of us. (Or, considering my newly realized heritage, should I say, smarter than the rest of *you*?) Whether in business or medicine or technological inventions, it's often a Jew who is at the forefront, leading the way.

I'm also aware that many people find Jewish folks a bit irritating. Well, for a certainty, Jesus was a thorn in the side of many folks in

Israel. And He did warn that His followers would be hated by the world. So whether Jew or Christian, perhaps there are good reasons why the world has its feathers ruffled by the people of God.

I could feel just such an irritation bubbling up among the passengers and flight attendants as we boarded the El Al flight in Paris.

A large contingent of Hasidic Jews were boarding the flight to Tel Aviv. It might be more proper to say there were a few Gentiles joining the Jewish flight. We were definitely in the minority, even though my name was *Stutzman* and I supposedly had "the features."

Many of the young men had a unique hairstyle under their large, black hats. The curls of hair dangling along the sides of their heads are called *payot*. This style, also known as *side curls,* follows the Old Testament command not to cut the hair at the corners of one's head. The instructions, if you're interested in reading it for yourself, are found in Leviticus 19, verse 27.

These fellows, dressed in black and white and wearing wide-brimmed black hats, could easily have strolled through my native Amish Country and fit right in—except for those long side curls.

As we boarded, the young men milled about, attempting to change seats, to the chagrin of the flight attendants. Older side-curled men stood awaiting assistance for seat switching as well. Some had been assigned a seat next to a woman, but they couldn't sit beside a woman who was not their wife. Sometimes the lady understood and obliged to the move. In other instances, an attendant needed to intervene and facilitate the move.

Once seated, the next matter of complaint was the food. We heard comments that the food wasn't kosher, and thus could not be eaten. The airlines make kosher meals available, and they can be ordered before leaving the ground. Apparently some folks hadn't had the foresight to do that.

The 13th Disciple

It was a relief—to everyone, I think—when we finally got our flight of God's chosen people off the ground.

. . .

As I prepared for backpacking in Israel, I had asked Craig what kind of weather to expect. Specifically, I wanted to know: *Do I need my waterproof gear?* I hate hiking in the rain and the misery of being totally soaked while putting one foot in front of the other.

Craig assured me that rain gear was totally unnecessary. "You probably won't see a drop of rain this time of the year."

Our flight approached Tel Aviv, and we landed in a rain storm. Disembarking on the runway, where a lineup of busses awaited to take us to customs, I sloshed my way to the bus and wondered what other misinformation had been fed to me.

We had reservations and checked in at the Abraham Hostel Tel Aviv, a large hostel with over 350 beds. Located at a busy downtown intersection, it's a central base from which to explore. From a rooftop lounge six or seven stories up, we had great views over the city. Tours to many attractions could be booked in the lobby, and we made arrangements for transportation to Nazareth the following morning.

CHAPTER 2

Born in a Barn

Israel is a small country. You can drive the entire width, east to west, in two hours. Top to bottom, the north-south length, in five hours. Even though Israel is small, all of its larger neighbors feel the country is too big—at least two-hours-by-five-hours too big.

Mind boggling. Those words came to mind the next morning as I watched the passing landscape from the window of the van headed toward Nazareth. Craig and I were crammed into the front seat, and I watched the signs along the road announcing names of Biblical towns that I'd heard hundreds of times, sitting in a church in Ohio and having no idea where, for example, Nazareth was in relation to Bethlehem. I saw a sign that told me Nazareth was seventy kilometers ahead. I was actually going to the town where Jesus was raised. *Mind boggling.*

Craig interrupted my reverie.

"This is the valley of Jezreel. We're passing through the Plains of Megiddo, where the battle of Armageddon will take place." How often I'd heard preaching about Armageddon, the final battle when the armies of the world meet to fight it out. Things won't be going well for the good guys until, finally, God swoops in and the battle is won for humanity. That short summary is probably missing some details; perhaps your pastor can fill those in for you.

"What do you hope to learn from your trip here in Israel?" asked Craig.

Could I give voice to all that had been floating through my cranium? I determined to try.

"Well," I began, "I'm hoping to discover who Jesus was. Did Jesus' life and history actually happen as the Bible says it did? Jesus was either who He said He was—the Son of God and the Messiah—or He was a mental case."

Does even the suggestion of such a question shock you? Isn't this really the bottom line? We read that Jesus' brothers even thought He had delusions. And at times, His own disciples doubted and found things hard to understand. They were *there,* with Him, and they had questions. Can you blame anyone two thousand years removed from that time for having doubts?

I was just getting warmed up. I wanted this ex-Marine to have a clear picture of the perils of being born into a heaping pile of Christianity.

"See, while many folks are born sinners, I arrived into this world a born-again Christian."

Of course, I don't really believe that, but the radical statement did give Craig pause and allowed me to continue. I was gaining momentum.

"I come from a heritage that many would consider fortunate, blessed even. However, that also comes with some difficulties."

I can imagine my dad explaining the plan of salvation to me on the day I was born: "Son, quit your crying and listen to what I have to say." (I was probably crying, since I weighed one ounce short of ten pounds and the journey had been difficult, not to mention what Mom went through.) But Dad most likely ignored my wails and went on, "Jesus died for your sins, and to qualify for Heaven and avoid the eternal fires of hell, you need to accept Jesus into that little heart of yours."

Yes, that is an exaggeration, but as soon as any of us children could formulate thoughts or words—no, even before we were able to speak—we heard stories and songs about Jesus and God and what God wants of us.

So, as I grew, I obeyed my parents, followed church rules, and actually was quite a good boy. That is, until I wasn't. That part comes later.

As I approached the age of better understanding, I heard the preachers remind us that we needed to turn from our sins and turn to Jesus. Many of my friends found their way to the altar and made some statement of faith. I felt kind of left out. I felt I had no real need to turn from anything, since I had not done anything too devious. Where was the sin I needed to turn away from? Not in my life. We had no radio or television; we were protected from those corrupting influences. My obedience might have been flawed by just a few misdemeanors, but none that I believed approached the "sin" level.

My birth had landed me in a family tree laden with preachers and mission-minded folk. My memories of my three uncles who were pastors include their ability to repeat an amazing number of Bible verses from memory. They impressed me with the importance and benefit of studying and knowing Scripture.

I can still hear my Uncle Roman, in his distinctive style of delivery, quoting Psalm 84:5-7:

The 13ᵗʰ Disciple

Blessed are those whose strength is in you, whose hearts are set on pilgrimage. As they pass through the Valley of Baka, they make it a place of springs; the autumn rains also cover it with pools. They go from strength to strength, till each appears before God in Zion.

I heard him quote that verse often at family reunions and finally at his wife's funeral service. The Valley of Baka was a place folks would pass through on their pilgrimage to Jerusalem. It was a dry, foreboding place. However, their faith turned this barren valley into a wellspring of joy. I believe Uncle Roman had discovered the secret of finding strength and joy when going through difficult situations.

Another one of my dad's brothers, Uncle Andrew, was the pastor of our church during my youth. He was a powerful preacher and had memorized entire chapters of the Bible. One of his favorites to quote at family reunions and from the pulpit was Psalm 16:5-6:

Lord, you have assigned me my portion and my cup; you have made my lot secure. The boundary lines have fallen for me in pleasant places; surely, I have a delightful inheritance.

The boundary lines Uncle Andrew was thinking of, I'm quite certain, were his Godly father and mother and the Christian heritage that had been passed down from his ancestors.

At age ninety-six, my Uncle David is my last living uncle. Recently, during a conversation we had at a reunion, he shocked me with this remark: "I have been a pastor for many years. I cannot remember a time I didn't believe in Jesus." He couldn't even recall the day he had made a decision to follow Jesus. I don't know why this surprised me so much. I had similar thoughts. I can't remember a time when I didn't believe the things I read and was told about Jesus.

I was just having trouble knowing what it means to believe *in* Jesus. And what does He mean when He says, "Follow me"? What does He require of us? Is it difficult or is it easy?

My dad taught us Bible verses, too. I recalled those from Matthew 11:28-30:

> "Come to me, all you who are weary and burdened," (Dad taught us "weary and heavy laden;" he was a King James kind of man), "and I will give you rest. Take my yoke upon you and learn from me, for I am gentle and humble in heart, and you will find rest for your souls. For my yoke is easy and my burden is light."

"It sure doesn't seem easy and light to me at times. Why not?" I said mournfully to Craig as I finished my long soliloquy. Did he understand? Had I clearly conveyed the questions that had me groping for answers?

"That's easy," he said, surprising me. "You were born in a barn."

That got my attention.

"I was a tough Marine," Craig went on. "I was like a wild stallion, running free with no restrictions. Untamed. One day, a chaplain explained my need for a relationship with Jesus. Like a wild horse, I didn't actually like the idea of a saddle being put on me or a bridle telling me which way to go. However, things changed me. My will for living a sinful life was broken, and I accepted Jesus. My life changed." It had indeed. He became a pastor.

"You," he went on, "were a colt born in a barn. You never ran wild. You followed your parents and mimicked them. Yes, a colt will resist briefly when weight is placed on its back, but it quickly succumbs. You were born into the rules of the barn, born into obedience. It's all you knew. You never had to decide whether or not to accept a saddle and bridle."

I liked Craig's comparison. My hiking partner seemed to have lots of horse sense.

He was right. I'd been born into the barn of obedience. I'd said the words all my life. Now I wanted to understand what I'd chosen and learn to better know the Man I claimed to follow.

. . .

God sent the angel Gabriel to the village of Nazareth to deliver a message, then (as far as we know), Gabriel left town. I was also sent to Nazareth—to *receive* a message. Then I, too, left town.

Of course, in that van, talking with Craig about barn-born colts and wild horses, I had no idea what awaited me in Nazareth.

During my wife's last days on this earth, my pastor encouraged me to look for signs from God intended only for me. One of those messages came on the night of my wife's funeral. She had loved Monarch butterflies; and that evening, as I dozed in my chair, a Monarch butterfly emerged from a chrysalis that had been attached to one of the floral arrangements sent by a friend. It was a message for my weary heart—an assurance that my wife had shed her earthly shell and had been transformed into a new creature.

As I began my search for the Jesus who lived and died here in Israel, another message would be delivered to me, up ahead, in Jesus' hometown.

CHAPTER 3

Room Number 13

The streets of Nazareth were narrow, and the buildings edged in closer and closer until our van finally braked to a stop. It could no longer squeeze between the buildings.

Our destination was the Fauzi Azar Inn, 6108 St., Nazareth, 16125.

That's possibly more of an address than the angel Gabriel had when he went searching for Mary's house with a life-changing message. "Just go to Nazareth, and she's at that square, brown, mud-encased building. You can't miss it." That might be all he had to go on. Well, I suppose, on a divine mission of that nature, Gabriel's global positioning was spot on. He undoubtedly had no trouble finding the right place.

"Is Mary home?"

"Who's there?"

"Gabriel."

"Gabriel who?"

"Gabriel, the archangel."

Do you suppose Mary cracked the door a bit to see who this unannounced visitor was?

"I was down in Jerusalem six months ago, and gave your relatives Zechariah and Elizabeth the news that they would have a baby boy," Gabriel told her. "Now I'm here to tell you that their little one is about to get a cousin."

Did the door open wide, then, or did the angel have to stand outside and deliver his message?

. . .

Let's allow Gabriel and Mary to continue their conversation while I get you caught up on other details of importance. We will get back to the house in Nazareth in due time. Before continuing to eavesdrop on that conversation, let us get checked in (assuming there is room at the inn) and help a lady in distress.

Since the buildings had pressed in upon us, the van could no longer continue up the narrow street. We were forced to ambulate the rest of the way to the inn.

A lady in our contingent had packed in one suitcase what must have been all of her earthly possessions. This monstrosity of implied movement had lost all mobility. The woman could have recovered the cost of travel by selling advertising on the suitcase's vast exterior.

One could not blame this container if it refused to roll or be lugged. Its handle was broken. Undoubtedly, some unfortunate handler who was now nursing a hernia had attempted to lift it.

Craig and I hoisted our own carefully planned packs to our backs. Unfortunately for us and to the great fortune of Mrs. Pack-all-things-materialistic, this also freed our hands. So I grabbed one end of the massive bag and Craig grabbed the other, and we gasped and wheezed our way uphill toward an awaiting bed—which we would need far sooner than we had anticipated.

This good-deed business also took us from the front of the check-in line to the far-off tail end.

One of my character traits that needs more polishing is patience. I may have a bit of a deficiency of patience. (Could my excess in other areas compensate for lack in this area?) Okay, I'll be blunt—I have no patience.

When I plan, I allow for this deficiency. For example, when I get in line to order food, I know what I want. Take my order. Dispatch me quickly. There'll be more sales for you, and your manager will be happy.

If it's not a line at a fast-food joint, it's a salad bar. Such set-ups are there to save time. Get seated, get up, get through the bar, eat, and leave. I admit, restaurant-manager mentality intensified this thinking, since the more table turns we got, the better our bottom line. As a salad-bar customer, I can go from plates (one end) to croutons and raisins (the opposite end) in thirty seconds. The problem is the lady in front of me who is surveying the gustatory landscape. She observes the lettuce, remarking that she would prefer it to be chopped into smaller pieces. She meanders along, stirring the dressing vigorously. I spot an opening on the other side of the salad bar and make a split-second decision to dart over to the other side. Too late. I get cut off at the pass. I can't take it any longer. I lay down my salad plate and leave in disgust.

When I'm driving: Hey, you-in-front-of-me! The traffic light is yellow. That means hurry up and go, so that I can get through, too.

Yes, this deficiency even shows up in church. And maybe this is a good place to say, "It's not my fault." Allow me to assign blame: My dad taught me this approach to life.

Dad was a man of order. Do things once, do them right. Don't be late to church or any other occasion, because tardiness shows a lack of respect. At one time, our church had a pastor who was notorious for going overtime, especially on Wednesday evening, prayer-meeting night. Closing time was 9:00 p.m. Without fail, the nine o'clock hour rolled around, and the pastor still had an allocation of words to unload. We young boys sat up in the front pews (only because taking our place there was a rite of passage.) One Wednesday evening, my father informed me that should the service go beyond nine o'clock again that evening, he would walk down the middle aisle, tap me on the shoulder, and we would be heading home. It did, and we did. Dad certainly made a point that evening. I admit that even now, as the minute for closing time of a church service approaches, I start feeling fidgety.

To me, these things are essential for a world of order: Know what you want, plan smartly, anticipate, and follow through. I've seen a poster that expresses my sentiments quite accurately: *Lead, follow, or get out of the way.*

So my plan on arrival at our inn in Nazareth had been to get to the front desk as quickly as possible and be checked in before anyone else's shadow even approached the entrance to the establishment.

But there I was, at the back of the line, chomping at the bit as I awaited access to my room. *Lord, I want patience, and I want it now!*

My impatience was interrupted by a conversation taking place at the check-in desk. The only people still in the lobby were the lady with the luggage monstrosity and her two porters, Craig and me.

I heard Craig say we needed two beds. We did have a room booked, but it seems the number of beds assigned to us was in dispute. The room we'd been given had only one bed. Mennonites and Marines do not sleep together in one bed! The lady previously in distress now came to our rescue and returned the favor we'd done for her.

"My husband and I only need one bed," she told the person behind the desk. "They can have our room with the two beds."

"That room also has a large TV," the innkeeper told Craig. "And it does cost a bit more than the one-bed room you currently have."

Wait, a television? Did I hear that correctly?

This was the evening of the seventh game of the World Series matchup of the Cleveland Indians and the Chicago Cubs. I, along with millions of other long-suffering Indians fans, had been waiting over sixty years for a World Series win. There I was in Nazareth, home of Jesus Himself, and I had the possibility of watching this game. Of course, there was a seven-hour time difference, so I needed to factor that into my sleep schedule.

The deal was made, and the room key was handed over. This was an actual key, with a round, dangling medallion attached to it. The medallion showed the room number. It was not only a room number, but it seemed like a friendly greeting from God Himself.

Room 13.

It was a message, a sign to me that I was once again right where I needed to be.

What I'm about to relate to you will cause some readers to question my sanity. I have no issue with that; I have the same question myself at times. However, hear me out.

There are folks that trust in numerology. I'm not one of those folks (although I do believe the number 7 represents completion, at least in Biblical terms.)

The number 13 has often carried connotations of evil or bad luck. Friday the 13th is considered an unlucky day. Some hotels will completely skip the thirteenth floor as they number the levels of their building. It seems to me that floor 14 would then in reality be floor 13. And there's even an official name for the fear that people have of the number 13: *triskaidekaphobia.*

A number of years ago, when my family was going through the valley of the shadow of cancer, the number 13 kept occurring frequently, popping up and grabbing my attention. It happened so often that I could not ignore it. An unusual number of license plates seemed to have that number. At stores or eateries, my change was often 13 cents. My change might even be $13.13—it happened more than once.

I spoke to close friends about this and discovered that they had had similar things happen in their lives. Several mentioned glancing at the odometers in their vehicles and seeing three or four identical numbers. They would take this as a sign from God that all was well, and each occurrence of "their number" gave them pause to thank God for anything and everything in their lives.

Of course, the general thought is that the number 13 is unlucky, and I was no different than most people. At first, I thought that this frequent sighting of 13 was God's reminder of how unlucky I was that my wife had cancer. Perhaps we had done something wrong, and this was my warning of impending doom. Yes, that's ridiculous, since I'm not the least bit superstitious. But when you go through trying times, you want answers.

Eventually, my thoughts did an about-turn, and I was determined to take 13 as my lucky—no, I'll use the word *blessed*—number. Now when I travel and stay in hostels, I'm often assigned bunk number 13. I take that as a reminder that no matter how alone I might feel, God has led me there, right to where He wants me to be at that time.

So at the Fauzi Azar Inn, I grabbed that Number 13 key and

rejoiced yet again with the knowledge that Israel was where God wanted me. Later, in our room (yes, there was a beautiful television), I told Craig my number 13 story. It was met with a great deal of skepticism. But a few days later, while we hiked between an olive grove and a major highway, Craig admitted he was almost convinced of the significance of 13 for me—he had also started to notice the number everywhere.

Let me say that I believe you could pick your own number, say, 12 or 16 or 99. You'll start seeing "your" number everywhere. It's up to you to decide what you believe about this, whether it's just pure coincidence or God actually speaking to us through such incidental details. I just know it's very comforting for me when 13 appears. I'm always reminded to thank God for His blessings to me and my family.

CHAPTER 4

Nazareth Village

Modern-day Nazareth has approximately seventy thousand inhabitants, making it the largest Arab town in Israel. Yes, the majority of the population is Muslim. Our inn was situated in what is known as the Old City, a section that still has the aura of an ancient town, with narrow and winding streets that were dirt up until the year 2000.

The inn, another one of the Abraham hostels, is a mansion built in the nineteenth century by the Azar family, an Arab family who had considerable wealth and influence in the city of Nazareth and the surrounding areas. The mansion stood empty and neglected for fifteen years toward the end of the twentieth century; then it was purchased by an Israeli couple who restored its original Ottoman architecture and turned it into a guesthouse, with the mission of creating a place where diverse faiths could live side by side and find community in spite of differences.

The owner of Fauzi Azar Inn is also a co-founder of the Jesus

Trail, which starts right outside the front door of the inn.

Many different walking trails wind their way through Jesus' homeland. Some are based on Biblical history and religious belief, like the Nativity Trail and Abraham's Path, and others are oriented more toward historical significance or geographical features of Israel, like the Israel Trail and the hike around the Sea of Galilee. Major trails are blazed with painted stripes on building walls, electric poles, rocks, and any other material suitable for a sprayed directional marker. Each trail has its own pattern of blazed colors. The Jesus Trail is marked by three ribbons of color: an orange stripe between two white stripes. At places where several trails run together, the marking for the Jesus Trail might be only an orange dot placed next to the blaze for another trail.

A route marked by purple circles meanders through the narrow streets, leading through a section called Nazareth Village, a re-creation of Jesus' hometown as it might have looked when He was a boy. The village exists to give visitors a sense of walking through the town that Jesus knew—a town that was probably only about three hundred people, give or take a hundred. Workers in Nazareth Village were dressed in period costumes and reenacted scenes common in daily life of Jesus' time. In one house, a lady explained how wool shorn from the sheep was turned into threads that were used to make clothing. A carpenter shop similar to the one where Jesus and His father might have worked displayed ancient tools and their use. A synagogue helped me imagine Jesus as a boy, studying the Torah, or Jesus at the beginning of His public ministry as He stood, one Sabbath morning, and announced that the prophecies about the coming of a Messiah were being fulfilled that very day. Sheep and goats, olive trees and grape presses, parables and farming stories— all created a glimpse into the world Jesus lived in as He grew into adulthood. Our tour guide, a young Christian Palestinian woman, expertly explained details of life at that time.

Nazareth Village is located on a hillside, and much of the surrounding rural area is terraced. Our guide pointed out the importance of everyone keeping their terraced walls in good repair. One section of wall neglected and crumbling would affect not only the property owner but his neighbor as well.

We passed a sheep pen filled with baaing sheep. Our guide explained how sheep recognize the shepherd's voice, a fact that Jesus referred to as He talked about being the Great Shepherd. One member of our tour group was from Germany, and she told of an incident in her community when a flock of sheep was being taken through an old village and somehow several of the sheep were separated from the flock and ended up trapped in a building. The residents of the building yelled at the animals, trying to shoo them outside, and the sheep panicked. Hearing the commotion, the shepherd turned back and called out to the sheep. The animals immediately recognized his voice and obeyed the command to follow him.

Stopping at an olive press, we watched a donkey trudging in circles, around and around. It was hitched to a wooden beam attached to a large millstone. Here, the olives were partially pressed before being moved to another area where three stones, each heavier than the last, were lowered to continue the pressing. The first pressing was gentle and produced pure olive oil. Each successive pressing with a heavier stone produced oils of a lesser grade. The oil resulting from the final pressing was usable only for burning in lamps.

The donkey's eyes were covered while it plodded in circles around the millstone. Our guide explained that this was done for the same reason that Samson had his eyes gouged out when the Philistines captured him and forced him to grind grain in the prison. The eyes were covered so that the donkey (and Samson) wouldn't get dizzy constantly going in circles.

In Jesus' day, Nazareth was considered a backwater town. Other towns looked down their noses at this small farming town. Some even questioned whether anything good could possibly come from this place.

But, of course, it did.

. . .

A man by the name of Joseph lived in this looked-down-upon town of Nazareth. Joseph was a good man. Indeed, he was a righteous man.

You probably know the story well, so you know where Joseph enters the narrative. We know very little about him after the accounts of Jesus' birth, but has it ever occurred to you that God must certainly have known that Joseph was the right man for the job of raising Jesus?

Joseph was betrothed to a young woman named Mary. Betrothal was a period of time that could be as long as one year between engagement and marriage. It was a binding contract between families—so serious and binding that a divorce would be needed to nullify the contract.

Speculation is that Mary's family lived in the neighboring town of Sepphoris, a town that had existed for centuries. It was situated on a hilltop, probably making it a desirable spot from which to command the surrounding area. The city had been ruled by Herod the Great, who built impressive structures, including his palace. When this Herod died, a Jewish group began a revolt against the Roman rule. The uprising was squashed, and a large part of the city was burned.

The city was being rebuilt during Jesus' time, and it could very well have happened that Joseph, a builder, met Mary while working in Sepphoris (although we also know that marriages at that time didn't follow our modern, boy-meets-girl-and-they-fall-in-love-and-get-married scenario).

I've always thought of Joseph as a carpenter, but carpenters build mainly with wood, and wood was a rare commodity in Nazareth. Lumber for roof trusses had to be shipped into town. Rock and stone were the most-used building materials.

So the word we've often used for Joseph—and Jesus, too—as *carpenter,* is probably misleading. Both men may have done some work in wood, but it's much more likely they were stone masons. The Greek word for *builder* is *tecton,* and what has been translated as *carpenter* is actually more accurate as *builder.*

In Sepphoris, only an hour's walk from Nazareth, huge stone structures were being built. We're not told in Scripture that Jesus and His father helped in the construction of some of those buildings, so that's merely speculation. Supporting this possibility is the fact that Jesus used a number of words that did not come from His Jewish upbringing but were probably picked up in His interactions with the non-Jewish culture in the neighboring town.

Many Jews did live in Sepphoris, but the culture was greatly influenced by Greek and Roman thought and by the commerce and wealth that shaped the town. We tend to forget that even in Jesus' time, the country was a jumble of Jewish and decidedly non-Jewish thought and lifestyles. Jesus was born into a society just as opposed to His message as our world is today. Except for a few segments of strict Jews who tried to withdraw completely and live apart from the rest of the world, Jesus' family, friends, and neighbors were exposed to and had to deal with "the world." They weren't living in a Jewish bubble.

The letters written to early Christian churches often speak of the need to guard against the influence of the world. We see reminders of this influence in the Gospels, too. For example, Herod had built a theater in the city of Sepphoris. The word *hypocrite* comes from a Greek term meaning *actor* or *deceiver* (as in the theater). This was not a word used by the Jews, but Jesus often used the term. Matthew 6, for instance, uses it three times in one chapter, but it was a word foreign to His own religious tradition.

I grew up knowing only about the divine Jesus, believing Him to be fully divine, with all His utterances directly from God. Now I was beginning to see His human side, as the sometimes strange combinations of circumstances in His life led to incongruities, which may seem small to you but helped me to see Jesus as a human like us. In His use of the word *hypocrite,* I see Him as a young man from a backward town, working in the worldly city, and picking up some of that language, which He then used to make a point in some of His own teachings.

. . .

Back to Joseph and Mary.

Mary may or may not have been born in Sepphoris, but by the time we meet her in accounts in Scripture, she has moved to Nazareth. It's likely that her betrothed, Joseph, had prepared a home for her and she had already moved there.

Jesus often used references to houses and homes in His teachings—another natural result, probably, of His knowledge of the building trade. He spoke of the importance of choosing a solid foundation when building, and declared that a house divided against itself cannot stand. He told a story about a woman sweeping her house to find a coin, and another time made a reference to an unclean spirit returning to the "house" it had left. We read about friends tearing up a roof to lower a man to Jesus, who was teaching below, and our modern minds wonder about the hole they must have made.

So it might be useful to understand a bit about house construction during the time of Jesus, here in Nazareth, where He lived, studied, and worked for almost three decades.

I know you're eager to start down the Jesus Trail—as was I—but linger just a bit longer with me here in Nazareth and attempt to see Jesus, the child, the teenager, the young man, working beside His earthly father in a common occupation, living an ordinary life according to Jewish traditions in a small, insignificant town.

In first-century Nazareth, there were several different types of house construction. It was not uncommon for the poor to build a structure that extended out from a cave in a hillside. A simple construction like this made the cave part of the "house," and used the natural cooling of the cave as an ancient air conditioner. In Bethlehem, the site designated as the place of Jesus' birth is actually a cave.

However, Joseph, the builder, had most likely prepared a house common in that era. Houses were usually built around an open courtyard, the area where cooking was done and the family shared life (like our current-day "family rooms" or "great rooms"). Individual rooms with roofs extended off this common area. Often, several generations lived in the same compound.

If animals were part of a household, they would be housed in a section of this structure. When we left Nazareth and walked toward Cana, I witnessed a house still employing this floorplan. The animals were within the walls of the house, separated from the living quarters by a simple partition.

This open-court design required smaller beams for the roof construction and also allowed air movement throughout the rooms. Although flat, the roofs had a slight incline so that rain water would drain off and be stored in the cistern, usually located in the courtyard.

A stairway led from the courtyard to the rooftop. You'll remember the story about the Shunammite woman who noticed that the prophet Elisha often traveled through town. She asked her husband if they could put a simple room on their rooftop so that the prophet would have a place to stay. It was a B.C. hostel.

The roof was also a place to socialize in the evening, when the day cooled off. Laundry was put up on the roof to dry during the day. Peter (among others) went up to the roof to pray. To reinforce the flat roofs so that they'd be strong enough to handle the activity of humans, a mixture of straw mats were tightly compacted and covered with hard clay between the trusses.

Roofs were so much a part of daily living that the Old Testament law (given in Deuteronomy) required that guard rails be installed to keep folks from falling off.

The walls of houses were typically limestone, laid up and covered with a stucco-like material. Floors were often bare ground, beaten down to a smooth surface. Some families with more resources available used baked clay tiles for flooring.

In areas where limestone was not readily accessible or if the owner was too poor to afford it, a house could be constructed out of mud bricks up to three feet thick. This type of construction would need a lot of attention and maintenance since rain could soften the walls. The houses made of clay were also a temptation for robbers. They would simply dig through those three feet of softened clay and do a home invasion. *Mud digger* was actually the Greek definition of *burglar*.

. . .

The angel Gabriel found Mary in Nazareth.

During our time in Israel, Craig would search the Scripture for readings appropriate for each location we visited. In Nazareth, he read Luke's account of God sending the angel Gabriel to this town—where I was now standing!—to deliver a very important message.

God had searched His creation for a highly favored woman to be the mother of Jesus. The candidate was found in that little, looked-down-upon town of Nazareth. Gabriel was sent "to a virgin pledged to be married to a man named Joseph, a descendant of David" (Luke 1:27). Her name was Mary, and the angel greeted her with strange words: "Greetings, you who are highly favored! The Lord is with you" (verse 28).

Can you visualize Mary's reaction to all of this?

About six months before, Gabriel had been sent to the priest Zechariah to give him a similar message: He would have a son, whose mission would be to prepare the way for the Messiah who was coming!

Mary answered the door, and she had the same reaction as Zechariah had when the stranger announced who he was: Fear!

Gabriel quickly calmed both Zechariah and Mary with the same words: "Do not be afraid." He went on to give her the astounding message: She would give birth to a baby boy who would be the Son of the Most High, and He would be a king who would rule forever.

I stood in the streets of Nazareth, imagining the scene unfolding at Mary's house as the angel explained why God had sent him. Whether in Greek, Hebrew, King James, or the NIV, the message was clear: Things were about to change!

CHAPTER 5

Call to Prayer

I was looking forward to finding out if this Promised Land was actually the land of milk and honey. (I'd always had a difficult time understanding that metaphor. I disliked milk, and so a land flowing with it didn't seem at all appealing to me.)

Recalling how I had longed to take communion during the time of my walk on the Camino de Santiago—and was usually denied the opportunity—I wondered if I would be fortunate enough to be invited to share a Shabbat dinner. *Shabbat* is the Jewish holy day of rest, beginning at sundown on Friday night and continuing until sundown on Saturday. Three meals are traditionally part of Shabbat: Friday night, Saturday noon, and late afternoon on Saturday. The Friday evening meal is a feast, or so I had heard. Would we be guests at a Shabbat dinner? Or were those special meals also forbidden to me, a non-Jew?

Craig and I left the inn and went in search of eating spots, following a narrow, winding alley. The first restaurant we found looked a bit too pricey for our pocketful of shekels.

Yes, indeed, *shekels*. That currency is still in use in Israel. When I had approached the teller at my local bank branch and asked for the exchange rate on shekels, she looked like she was waiting for the punch line to a joke. (I often go in there with a smart-aleck comment; she was probably banking on that fact.) After assuring her that I was serious, she made a quick phone call to the main bank in a neighboring town and confirmed that twenty-seven American dollars would garner me about one hundred shekels.

Our second choice of eateries had every table in the dining room booked for a tour group. Come back in an hour, and we can seat you, they said. Craig and I agreed there was no chance we were going to do that.

Then we approached a small deli squeezed into a building, with the main "dining room" consisting of tables and chairs outside, almost on the street. An old man was seated at one table, his portly body spilling over every edge of the chair that miraculously held him aloft. The establishment was tiny and he was not, and our view of the offerings inside was blocked. He took a big draw on his pipe, saw our curiosity, and informed us in broken English that this place had the best food in town.

The middle-aged proprietor ambled out and invited us in for a sample of his wares. First, we inquired of two gentlemen seated at another table whether the food they were eating had been purchased inside. It had, and they reported that it was delicious.

If you've ever been to a Greek restaurant you may have seen meat skewered in a vertical position and revolving on a spit. It slowly rotates round and round, and the chef slices off pieces as needed. This shop was not much bigger than two phone booths spliced together, but it had two of these rotisseries, along with a buffet and a deli counter.

The proprietor recommended a pita stuffed with lamb. I simply won't eat lamb, for the same reason I won't eat dog, cat, or horse meat. Yes, I do eat pigs and chickens. I didn't say my choices make sense.

"No lamb!" I exclaimed, shaking my head.

"Oh, this one here is beef," he replied, in English.

"I'll take a beef pita, then."

We seated ourselves at a table outside to wait for the main course to arrive. In the meantime, the owner's young son kept a parade of goodies flowing out the door to our table. I had the first of the many salads I would consume in the days to come—yes, salads for breakfast, lunch, and dinner was the norm for my time in Israel. I enjoyed the fresh pickles, tomatoes, cabbage, roasted peppers, and, of course, the delicious breads that were always served.

One plate the young waiter placed in front of me held nothing but a greenish-brown paste.

"What's this?" I asked Craig, eyeing the stuff. He told me it was hummus. To my thinking, it looked like a smashed pile of Little Marvel peas. I was partially correct.

In the States, we serve chickpeas on salad bars. Did you know that? Probably not. They're mostly overlooked as one peruses the salad bar. Chickpeas are also called *garbanzo beans,* and they're those little, brownish-white round beans. Hummus, it turns out, is simply chickpeas that have gone high society.

Smash chickpeas into a puree, add tahini (a sesame paste), garlic oil (which will improve any dish), and a dash of lemon juice, and you have hummus. Hummus might arrive surrounded by a plethora of vegetables. Make no mistake, however, the hummus is the main attraction. Yes, it's a bit of an acquired taste, but my experience in Israel was that some hummus was good and other hummus was great. The choice of ingredients is what enhances a hummus. If I learned nothing else in twenty-five years of restaurant management, I did learn this: Plenty of sugar, butter, or garlic can make just about any food palatable.

That evening, a great bread enhanced my introduction to hummus, and that greenish paste (with accompaniments) would also be part of my diet three times a day for the duration of my time in Israel.

The beef pita arrived, along with more fresh vegetables—chopped lettuce, cabbage, peppers, and red beets. And more delicious bread.

. . .

Another difficultly I've had is understanding prayer. How about you? Do you ever feel as though your prayers go nowhere? How can God hear every prayer uttered in the same moment I'm praying? How can we communicate with someone we've never seen? Do you visualize God when you're talking to Him? Have you figured out how to "pray without ceasing," as the apostle Paul advocates? Do you sometimes feel as though God's response to you might be, "Oh, why are you bothering me with *that?*"

In spite of my questions and inadequate understanding, I think I've always known that prayer is a mystery, a connection that God gives us to Himself. For all of my life, since I was a frisky little colt in the barnyard, I've known how important prayer is. But yet, my prayer life would often begin late in the evening, and then I'd kneel at my bed—and soon fall fast asleep.

Did the few thoughts I had before falling asleep on my knees go anywhere? Can a person think a prayer that God can hear or does it need to be spoken? And if a thought prayer can be heard by God, doesn't that mean He can also hear all our thoughts? So why do we pray aloud?

We were always taught to pray with our eyes closed. I know that when I and my sisters were young, Dad would often raise his head a bit and open one eye, peeking at us to see if we all had our eyes closed in prayer. The fact that I know this tells you the position of my own eyelids.

We are told all these things about prayer, and we take them by faith—because that is what barn-born Christians do.

I suppose we close our eyes as a way to avoid distraction, but I've found that it doesn't block all the distractions from within my own mind. As a matter of fact, some of my best praying has been done with eyes wide open, strolling through a wooded area or along a busy street.

My time in Israel gave me many reasons to think about my prayer connection to God.

The Jews I met on my journey were very open about their prayer life. And whatever one thinks about Muslims, they too are people of prayer.

Five times a day, those of the Muslim faith are called to prayer by an announcement from a minaret. The *muezzin* is a man who chants or drones or sings—I'm not even sure which word is most accurate—specific lines to summon Muslims to prayer. This is called the *adhan*. Traditionally, a muezzin would climb the stairs to the top of the minaret to intone, at the proper times, each adhan. In most cases now, towns use a recording blasted from a sound system in the top of the minaret. Some minarets are so tall that it would be impractical to have a person climb that many steps. As soon as the muezzin reached the sidewalk, it would be time to head back up the steps again to proclaim the next adhan.

The 13th Disciple

While Craig and I enjoyed our meal at the tiny eatery, our conversation was interrupted by this summons to pray. It was the first time I'd heard it.

Some folks think this call to prayer is wonderful to listen to. Others find it annoying, especially the volume. The sound overrides anything else going on below. We'd be walking toward a town as the time for prayer approached, and we'd hear the call a mile away. I suppose the volume is turned way up so that even those on the edges of town are not missed. Or maybe there are folks (like me) who are in danger of sleeping instead of praying and need to be awakened.

Upon hearing the call to prayer, a Muslim will stop whatever activity he is involved in at the time and perform *wudu*. This is ablution, or washing of the body. It's a ceremonial cleansing that involves washing the mouth, eyes, ears, nose, hands, elbows, and feet. This washing with cold water awakens the senses and prepares the person to enter into fervent prayer.

The adhan lasts about four minutes and then an actual prayer follows that lasts about seven minutes. It reminded me of "Das Loblied," sung in my Amish community. This is a long, drawn-out song in which the male leader starts on one note and drags it out for a long, long time. Eventually the congregation joins in and every note is captured and has the life squeezed out of it. Long note by long note, the song is sung. There are jokes about sneaking out of the services and doing chores during the Loblied and still getting back in time to complete the song. The sound of the Muslim call to prayer is also similar to the sound of the Loblied—a haunting, somewhat tuneless and melancholy droning.

Although the words of the call to prayer are always the same, the sound will be different from one minaret (or one muezzin) to another, of course, like any song performed by different voices. The muezzin was often chosen because of his good vocals. However, instead of a congregation joining and assisting in the song, the muezzin sings all notes himself.

Whether or not the adhan is pleasing to a person's ears is dependent on one's understanding of what is being sung.

The call to prayer is as follows: "God is the greatest. God is the greatest. I bear witness that there is none worthy of worship except God. I bear witness that Muhammad is the messenger of God. Hasten to prayer. God is the greatest. God is the greatest. There is none worthy of worship except God."

There will be slightly different translations of that, since the summons comes in Arabic, and I'm writing in English. Oh, there's also another line added to the call to prayer that is sung before dawn: "Prayer is better than sleep."

I could bestow a good Mennonite *Amen* on many of those statements. And wouldn't it be a good idea for us Christians to have calls to remind us to be praying to the only One who is worthy of our worship? That might help some of us.

But this call to prayer won't work for Christians. Whether the Christian God and the Muslim Allah are one and the same is the subject of much discussion and controversy. There are people far better equipped than I to answer that question. To me, the issue is the choice of Jesus or Muhammad. Who will we follow? I believe Jesus is the only mediator between us and God. My choice is to follow Him. That's why I was in Israel. I was seeking to follow even more closely.

It seems to me that Christians are timid about prayer. Neither Jews nor Muslims that I met in Israel were apologetic or inhibited about their prayers. Especially in America, we have let the thinking creep into our practice that we don't want to be offensive to anyone observing us. Jews and Muslims have no such compunction.

Or is it that we're ashamed of being a follower of Jesus? In this world that hates Him, are we afraid to stand as His representatives?

I sometimes think I might be. I certainly don't want to be and don't intend to be. However, the disciple Peter would have declared the same, but when he was pressured, his actions denied his words. Are we like that? Yes, I plan to ask you tough questions, but I'll be peering into the mirror of introspection myself.

Luke 9:26 and Mark 8:38 are similar verses, both stating that if we are ashamed of Jesus as we live out our allotted time in this sinful world, He will return the favor and be ashamed of us when we stand before Him. I like Matthew 10:32 better. It presents the positive perspective, assuring us that whoever acknowledges Jesus before men will be acknowledged by Jesus.

Before we ate, we acknowledged our allegiance. We bowed our heads and Craig offered a vocal prayer.

Why do we pray before we partake of meals? Simply because we were taught to do so? What if we would make the act of taking sustenance be our own call to prayer—a true, authentic prayer instead of a ritual? After all, we eat in answer to a "call" of our stomachs or some other trigger in our brain. Might it also serve as a reminder to praise the one and only Great God? Or could you use something else as your call to prayer? Some folks set reminders on their smart phones or watches. Could it be the chimes of a clock in your house that remind you to connect with your Heavenly Father? Or every time you need a drink of water? Is there something in your days that occurs at regular intervals that you can make your own summons to pray?

. . .

Seated at the table next to us were the two men who had recommended the place. They overheard Craig's prayer and then heard us talking about the next morning when we would begin our hike on the Jesus Trail.

"You fellows must be Christians," one said, "and what's the Jesus Trail?"

That's how we became acquainted with Mike and Lee from Boca Raton, Florida, via South Africa.

The two gentlemen introduced themselves, and although their English was perfect, it was marked by a very pleasant accent. They were both born and raised in South Africa before coming to the States. South Africa has eleven officially recognized languages, one of which is Dutch. As we continued our conversation, Mike and Lee's accent attracted the attention of an elderly couple. They seemed to be more interested in the accent than in our actual conversation.

"Are you men from South Africa?" the lady wondered. "We recognized your accent."

The couple had been missionaries for many years in different countries, including South Africa, with their most recent ministry in Afghanistan. They were natives of the Netherlands, and she told us that her grandfather had built the house in Haarlem (a town near Amsterdam) in which Corrie ten Boom had been raised.

Mike and Lee were both hikers. Mike had been hiking the Israel National Trail, a trail that runs the entire length of Israel, north to south, 680 miles. (Anyone attempting this hike is well advised to do considerable research; there are stretches of desert hiking where the water supply is minimal to none. Preparations need to be made for water caches along the way.) He was well into his hike when he received a call from his friend Lee, who had abruptly quit his job and wanted to join him on the trail. Lee had just arrived in Israel the previous day, had put in a long day of hiking, and now had two feet that were so badly blistered that he could hardly walk.

Lee had been working on a yacht for a very wealthy land developer, but he was going through a rather rough stretch in life. His broken marriage and the recent murder of his mother by his stepdad had brought him to a breaking point. It was the catalyst, though, for Lee to turn his life around. He searched the Scriptures and soon realized the lifestyle that surrounded him on the rich man's yacht was not conducive to Christ-like living. He, too, was desiring to understand more fully the true meaning of following Jesus.

CHAPTER 6

Boyhood Years

I was in Nazareth, the boyhood home of Jesus. My mind knew this, yet it seemed impossible that the area I walked through was where Jesus had lived, maybe, as a boy, running through the same narrow streets with His buddies. This was where He had played, worked with His dad, and went to the synagogue for lessons with a teacher.

Is it not amazing that we do not know more about Jesus' childhood? He was the most famous man who ever walked upon the earth. Yet there has been more spoken and written about His birth than about the entirety of His first thirty years.

Following the birth of Jesus, His parents had Jesus circumcised and then made the trip to the Temple in Jerusalem to consecrate Him to the Lord, as required by Jewish law. A sacrifice was also offered at that time. We are not told precisely what that sacrifice was, but it was either a pair of doves or two young pigeons. This suggests to me that Joseph and Mary did not have great financial means—Levitical law said that a lamb should be brought, but if they could not afford a lamb, the birds were acceptable substitutes (Leviticus 12:8).

I have often said and written that I believe in God-ordained appointments. We do not "just happen" to cross paths with someone—God often has a purpose in what we might think are "chance" meetings. In the Temple, Mary and Joseph had two such meetings.

Luke tells us plainly that the first man the family met was led there by the Holy Spirit on that day, at the precise time the family was in the Temple. Simeon was an old man who had been watching for the fulfillment of the promise of a Messiah, and God had promised him he would not die until he had seen the Messiah. What a promise!

You readers who are parents, do you remember holding your baby in your arms, looking down at that tiny face and wondering what your child would be like in twenty years? What kind of woman would she grow up to be? What career might he choose?

Joseph and Mary stood amazed when Simeon took their baby into his arms and said, "I am seeing the Promised One of God. He will be a light to reveal God to the nations, and the glory of all Israel."

And just as Simeon said this, along came Anna, an elderly widow who was a prophet. She also began praising God for keeping His promise, and started talking to everyone about the Baby who was going to rescue the Jewish nation.

What could Joseph and Mary have been thinking and talking about as they left the Temple that day?

I wouldn't be surprised if they were saying, *How can this possibly be? How can it ever happen?*

· · ·

The Gospels give us only a small glimpse into the boyhood years of Jesus, as He grew up in Nazareth. Luke 2:40 says that Jesus grew and became strong and was filled with wisdom, and the grace of God was upon Him. Luke 2:51 says He obeyed His parents. I tried to imagine Him as a boy, helping in the courtyard of their home, roaming the narrow streets and hills of the small town with His friends, and—I like to think—walking through the wonders of nature and enjoying His Father's great creation. If indeed He became a builder and worked with stones and rock, physical strength would have been a natural result of such hard work. Yes, my carpenter friends, I know that slinging those shingles and drywall boards will strengthen one as well.

The next mention we have of Jesus is the account of another trip to Jerusalem, when He was left behind in the Temple during the Feast of the Passover. This was a yearly pilgrimage the family made, traveling with numerous friends and relatives from Nazareth.

It's time for a quick geography lesson.

Jesus' life and ministry took place in three areas of the land known as Palestine. To avoid confusion, I'll refer to Palestine by its more commonly used name, Israel.

The northern part of Israel was Galilee. The towns of Nazareth, Cana, and Capernaum were located here. Cana is a short hike from Nazareth, about eight or nine miles. Sepphoris lies between the two towns. Two days' hike (about thirty-five miles) from Nazareth is Capernaum, on the shores of the Sea of Galilee. Several major trade routes passed through Capernaum. When Jesus left Nazareth at age thirty to be baptized by John the Baptist, He then returned to Galilee and located his ministry in that busy town by the sea.

The southern portion of Jesus' travels was the area known as Judea. The towns of Jerusalem, Jericho, Bethany, and Bethlehem were located there. Again, just to give you some perspective, Jerusalem was about seventy miles from Capernaum. That's three very long days of walking, more likely four or five days. (With the exception of Jesus' ride into Jerusalem, we never read of Him using transportation other than His two feet, but He might have, at times.) A trip to Jerusalem for the family would have been, at the very least, a three-day trek.

In between Galilee and Judea lay Samaria. The inhabitants of this area were also of Jewish descent, but their history had taken other turns than that of Judea, and Judean Jews viewed the Samaritans with great dislike and open hostility. The Samaritans, in Jerusalem's eyes, had corrupted Jewish traditions, beliefs, and theology. Jews wanted nothing to do with the "renegade" Samaritans, and the feeling was mutual. It was in Samaria that Jesus broke every social rule and not only talked to a woman in public, but a Samaritan woman! This history of feuding and antagonism makes the actions of the Samaritan who stopped to help his enemy even more remarkable. (And it's also important to note that Jesus' talk with the Samaritan woman opened the door for Him in that town—John recorded that they were very receptive to Jesus' teaching and many of them believed in Him.)

When anyone from Galilee needed to travel to Jerusalem, they had a choice of three routes. They could follow the coastline south, along the western border of Samaria; or they could travel along the eastern edge of Samaria, where the Jordan River formed a natural valley (today this is the dividing line between the countries of Israel and Jordan); or they could take the least desirable route, right through the heart of Samaria. This was the shortest and quickest route, and ran over mountain passes. But if they could, Jews avoided this, because of the tension between the Jews and the Samaritans. Again, knowing this, I find it all the more remarkable when Jesus was leaving Jerusalem for Galilee and told His disciples that He "had to" go through Samaria. It might have been because this was a faster route, but I believe it was probably because He knew He had an appointment at the well with the Samaritan woman.

So we can imagine the caravan of folks going to Jerusalem for the Feast of the Passover. Every time they went to Jerusalem and then traveled back home to Galilee, they needed to decide what route they would take. If, by necessity, they chose the mountain passes of Samaria, they undoubtedly traveled together, for the safety in numbers.

At the end of the first day of traveling back to Galilee, Jesus' parents realized He was not in the group. They had probably assumed He was with His group of friends (twelve-year-olds like to hang out together, and they knew they had days to travel). But no one had seen Jesus.

Joseph and Mary went in frantic search, returning to Jerusalem (another day's journey), and discovered He had stayed behind in the Temple. They walked in to find Him talking with the Jewish teachers. A twelve-year-old!

"Why would you bother looking for me?" He asked. "Are you not aware that I must be in my Father's house?"

That response might have different meanings. It could be construed as a question requiring an answer. Or it might have been a statement, such as, *Surely you know I'm right where I need to be.*

Perhaps Mary realized it. Mary had been doing a lot of pondering as Jesus grew up. As for Joseph—well, I can't imagine Joseph not realizing they had a special child. The circumstances surrounding His birth had amazed them. Doubtless both of them often thought of Simeon and Anna's words and wondered what the future held for their son.

The 13ᵗʰ Disciple

. . .

Most Jewish boys started memorizing the written Torah at a young age. By the time Jesus was conversing with the rabbis in the temple at age twelve, He would have already memorized Genesis, Exodus, Leviticus, Numbers, and Deuteronomy. These five books from what we call the Old Testament are also known as the five books of Moses. Another common term in Christian circles is the *Pentateuch*. Since class is still in session, you might as well learn the Greek origin of the word: *penta* is the word for *five, teukhos* means *books*.

Besides the written law, numerous laws and regulations in the Jewish tradition were passed down verbally, from generation to generation. This body of tradition was known as the Oral Torah. These were directives regarding everyday living, such as dietary habits, festival observations, agricultural practices, civil suits, and other guidelines for living.

The synagogue was the focal point in any Jewish town. It functioned much like a modern-day community center. Schools were often held in synagogues, and that's where Jesus would have done His reading and study of the Torah. Remember that most learning in Jesus' time was done by oral repetition. Although there were scrolls of sacred writings, books did not exist. Children started memorizing Moses' writings at a young age.

It was normal for men to get married before reaching the age of twenty; however, it was not uncommon for scholars seeking to become rabbis to postpone marriage until later in life, in order to concentrate on their studies. Rabbis were teachers, those who had studied the law and the Torah far beyond the ordinary person. Jesus was apparently studying to be a rabbi, and throughout the Gospels we have people recognizing Him as one having that training and knowledge. We also hear Jesus often quoting the Old Testament writings. He knew His stuff. It is believed that Jesus continued studying the Scriptures up until the age of thirty, when His ministry began. This makes things all the more dramatic, too, when Jesus says, "You have heard it said … *But I say* …" He was bucking the establishment. He wasn't following tradition or *the rules*. He was spreading new teaching that He claimed came directly from God.

But I'm getting ahead of myself.

Occasionally some farfetched theory is floated that perhaps Jesus had married someone, but no evidence of that exists, either in Scriptures or accounts from historians of the day. The real truth is that Jesus will be married, He is waiting for His bride, and there will be a great wedding feast. You and I are invited to be active participants at this wedding (Revelation 19:6-9).

From the age of eight days to age thirty, when Jesus started His ministry with being baptized in the Jordan by his cousin John the Baptist, we have only that small glimpse of Him in the Temple in Jerusalem and the statement in Luke 2:52 that Jesus grew and increased in wisdom and stature, both with God and man. One more small detail pops up in Luke 4. Luke states that Jesus went to the synagogue, "as was His custom." He was a regular. Those snippets are all that the Scriptures reveal about the first thirty years of Jesus' life.

Can you imagine any president, king, or ruler in the history of mankind with that little known about their first thirty years? We can, however, speculate what Jesus' life might have been like as He grew up here in Nazareth. Archaeology has told us what houses looked like. Historical accounts give us a picture of the ruling class and politics of the day. We know about foods and grains available for sustenance, and the ways in which people made a living.

The 13th Disciple

Walking the old streets of Nazareth caused me to think more than ever before about Jesus as a boy, a teenager, and then a young man, growing up there, gaining wisdom and strength, preparing for a teaching ministry. I wonder when He knew that this was what He was meant to do with His life?

CHAPTER 7

Jesus the Man

"Anyone who has seen me has seen the Father!"

Jesus spoke those words to the disciples on His last night with them. John wrote in his gospel that Jesus was God. Yet Jesus also talked about the Father being greater than He was and that He had come to do His Father's will. We know that Jesus spent much time praying, praying, and praying to the Father. A third Person is also part of the narrative—the Holy Spirit, and we sometimes refer to Him as the Spirit of God or the Spirit of Christ. How do these three all exist as God, and yet exist separately?

I can't explain it. It's beyond our experience or the ability of our minds to understand it. The Trinity is a mystery that we accept by faith.

Another mystery: How could Jesus have been fully human and also fully divine? I've grappled with that question since visiting Israel. While growing up, I put all the emphasis on His divinity—and completely missed His humanness. For most of my life, I imagined that Jesus was born as the Son of God and from His first breath had the wisdom of the world in Him. I now realize that if that were so, He would not have needed to spend time all those years, till age thirty, learning and memorizing the Old Testament.

When He was a young boy, what did His mother tell Him, if anything? What did His siblings know? Did Mary or Joseph ever tell Him about the strangers from the East who had come, bearing gifts, to find and worship a king? Did the husband and wife have discussions with each other, wondering what to tell their boy and what not to tell Him, or *when* to tell Him? Twice in one chapter, Luke tells us that Mary "treasured up" in her heart the remarkable events, first, those surrounding Jesus' birth, and then, the extraordinary conversations her son was having with religious teachers—when He was only twelve years old. Perhaps the idea that their son could be Israel's promised Messiah was such a shocking, incredible idea that Joseph and Mary did not talk about it even to each other.

Did the boy Jesus know that He was sent from God to accomplish a mission? Or did that all come as He studied the Scriptures, prayed, and trained to become a teacher? Maybe, even by the age of twelve, He was beginning to see the scope of what God the Father had planned for Him.

We don't know the answers to those questions. I believe we *can't* know the answers. At least, not in this life.

Throughout Jesus' life and ministry, we see both His humanity and His divinity, both natures often displayed in the same scene. It's interesting that Jesus announced in His hometown synagogue that "This day this Scripture is fulfilled," after He read prophecy about the promised Messiah, but Luke reports that even as He began His ministry, "Jesus was known as the son of Joseph" (Luke 3:23). Surely, people were seeing Him as a human being, the son of someone they knew, not as the Son of God. But shortly after, in one of Jesus' very first encounters with an evil spirit, the demon shouted, "I know who you are—you're the Holy One of God!"

How did humanity and divinity meet in one person? Were they both there, all along? Given what we now know about DNA, isn't it possible that when the Spirit of God began that baby's life within Mary, He implanted His own DNA, along with the building blocks of human life?

Does that sound shocking, even sacrilegious, to talk of God as having DNA and speaking of Him in human terms? But that is what God did. He took on DNA and everything else that makes us part of the human race—and He became one of us.

As I've said, our minds cannot resolve all these perplexities. Accepting that Jesus was both a man and God is a matter of faith. My time in Israel would enrich my faith by helping me see that Jesus was a man who knew the joys and sorrows we know, a man who felt the strong enticement of temptation, and a man who ate, cried, and grew weary.

It is not my intent to downplay or give any less importance to the fact that Jesus was God. This is central to my belief system: God came into the world as a human to rescue us. However, while Christians believe in Jesus' divinity, I am convinced that it's equally important to catch the significance that He was also *fully* a human being. He took on the nature—the mind, heart, will, and body—of a human just like us. And that is just as deep a mystery as the Trinity. How could He be 100 percent human and 100 percent God at the same time? Our minds say that's not possible. But Scriptures tell us that is what happened.

Why is it important for us to know the human Jesus? What difference does it make to my faith?

Well, if Jesus was God, only masquerading about as a human, then it was no big deal for Him to go through anything here on earth. He was God. He could handle anything, right? If He was God, He couldn't have died; God can't die. If He was God, what did physical pain mean to Him? Nothing. If He was God, He knew what The Plan was, and He knew that He was going to win in the end.

But as a human, Jesus experienced fully everything we must face. He felt joy and loneliness, hunger and pain. As God's will was moving Him toward death, He struggled with the very human reaction of wanting to avoid that if at all possible. He had a need for the strength that came only through prayer. He was often frustrated with people. And He came under the strong pull of temptation to do things His own way. Remember when He talked with His disciples about His death and Peter vehemently said that this *could not* happen? I'm sure Peter was just trying to be encouraging and optimistic, but Jesus was rather sharp with His friend. That's when He said, "Get behind me, Satan!" (What if the Lord would call you 'Satan'?) "You're a dangerous trap to me" (Luke 16:23). Jesus went on to say that Peter was only looking at things from a human point of view, not from God's perspective. But we hear in Jesus' words an admission that He *could* have been trapped by Satan's strategy of having a dear friend suggest something other than God's will.

So, since Jesus experienced everything we have, He understands exactly what we go through when we are sorrowful, tempted, weary, and dragging our feet when we should be following God's will. The writer of Hebrews tells us that even though He was God's Son, Jesus learned obedience through suffering (Hebrews 5:8). Did you catch that? He, too, had to *learn* to obey God, and those lessons came through the same kinds of suffering we meet.

He's been here, done this. *He knows.* When He tells His disciples and us that we will have trouble in this life, He knows exactly what it means for you or me to have to slog through a valley of trouble. When He tells us He can give us peace, He's not simply waving off the tumult and conflicts of life because He is God—no, He knows how chaotic life can be and how elusive a true peace might seem as we live out our allotted years here. He was born as one of a race who had suffered for generations under the rule of kings and emperors who did not share their values or their beliefs. He had no personal wealth, possessions, or home. The more He spoke in public, the more His message polarized even His own people. He was popular at first, but when folks started hearing more of His teaching, they were disenchanted and critical. The religious leaders viewed Him as troublesome and disruptive, and He knew they were cooking up schemes to silence Him. Even members of His family were embarrassed by Him. Jesus knows what *trouble* is like.

Scripture also tells us that Jesus had to be human to pay the price for human sins. He never sinned Himself, but to offer Himself to take the punishment for humanity's sins, *He had to be one of us.* His physical wounds, the things He suffered in His earthly, human body, made possible the healing of humanity.

A man died for me. A man who did not deserve to die. A man who was willing to die so that even His enemies could live.

God is God. I worship and reverence the Almighty Creator God. But I have chosen to *follow* a man.

. . .

Jesus' cousin, John, had been having revival meetings out in the wilderness by the Jordan River, exhorting people to repent and get ready because the Messiah was finally coming. Baptism was a sign of cleansing and repentance, and apparently the Teacher from Capernaum wanted to be baptized, too, so He made the trip to the Jordan River.

According to Mark 1, when Jesus came up out of the water, the heavens split apart and the Spirit of God descended on Him. John witnessed this and likened it to a dove landing on Jesus. Both Luke and Mark report that a voice came from Heaven, saying, "You are my dearly loved Son, and you bring me great joy" (Luke 3:22).

What a confirmation that was for the young Jesus of Nazareth who had been so diligent and devoted in His studying! Could that also have been an encouragement to strengthen Him for what He would have to face next?

. . .

Why God determined that the next forty days was a necessity for Jesus eludes me. However, the testing Jesus then went through was similar to testing we all face in life. And if I'm following in the footsteps of my Teacher, then there's probably something here that I need to learn.

The Spirit of God had descended on Jesus. God saw that His Son had completed the thirty years of human learning, and the time to enact His plan to save the world had arrived.

The Spirit "compelled" or "drove" (depending on the translation of the Bible you're using) Jesus to go into the wilderness to be tempted by the devil. We often call this period of time the "Temptation of Jesus." It was a test of Jesus' devotion to doing the will of His Father. Satan was out to lure Jesus away from His mission and God's plan.

Let's attempt to think about *the man* who was in the wilderness, meeting the devil.

He had just had this wonderful experience of baptism with the added bonus of an actual voice from Heaven that confirmed His identity and God's approval of Him. If you had a baptism experience like that, wouldn't you be elated? Feeling strong and sure of your call? I would.

I'm guessing that as a young man, Jesus had not had a personal, eyeball-to-eyeball encounter with Satan before this. At least, we're not told of such an encounter. Now, off in the wilderness by Himself, Jesus was shown exactly what He was up against. This was a direct spiritual attack by the enemy of God. Satan probably realized the threat Jesus posed.

We might think that of course Jesus could resist the devil's sneaky sales spiel. Again, this is an account that we tend to gloss over because we think, *Oh, Jesus was the Son of God. He could handle the devil. His hunger pains and the temptation of pride and power weren't temptations like I've got—those temptations that I think are almost impossible to resist. Jesus could handle it.*

No. I think Jesus struggled mightily with those temptations. Be assured, Satan knows the weaknesses of his targets. He's smart and he's powerful. He was once one of the elite angels. And he had a lot to lose if he allowed Jesus of Nazareth to get on with His teaching and ministry. He knew exactly who Jesus was, and I think he also knew that Jesus was a man—a man like I am. Satan appealed to those things in all of us humans that can lead us astray. Scriptures say Jesus struggled with the same temptations we have, in every area that we've been tempted (Hebrews 4:15). The lust of the flesh, the lust of the eyes, and the pride of life—those weapons would never have worked against God, and Satan knew it. He was aiming at Jesus' humanity.

Let's take a look at the details.

CHAPTER 8

Temptation and Rejection

In the wilderness, Jesus had nothing to eat for forty days. Surely His body was exhausted. We all know what hunger and exhaustion does to our thinking and our will.

Satan's very first strategy involved food. When Eve was tempted in the Garden of Eden, the food dangled in front of her appealed to her appetite, appealed to her visually, and appealed to her pride, in that she and her accomplice, Adam, were promised great wisdom.

When the children of Israel were wandering in the wilderness, their complaints about food also led to dire consequences. They wanted something different than what God supplied. But they lost what He had promised them.

Adam and Eve and the children of Israel had failed at the point of this human weakness. Now Satan brought another version of the same temptation into his challenges to Jesus. Knowing how hungry Jesus must have been, Satan told Jesus to turn the surrounding rocks into bread. Surely a simple enough thing for God to do! (This tells us that Satan is also aware that Jesus is the Son of God.) Satan is taunting Jesus. And after all, such a miracle would meet a need; Jesus was hungry.

Satan uses the same tactics today, appealing to our fleshly appetites. He attacks when we are "hungriest," weakest, and most apt to give in to those hungers.

Back when I was a youngster, in Bible School we often had a contest called a *Bible drill.*

"Bibles up!" the leader would yell, and all our Bibles were held aloft.

A Scripture reference was called out. "Micah 6:8!"

Our young minds were already running through the books of the Bible, attempting to place *Micah.*

"Go!" the leader called, and the first person to find the verse would stand up and read it.

I enjoyed the drill, except that there always seemed to be that kid who had a Bible with tabs marking the location of all the books. One glance at that Bible, and we kids whose parents couldn't afford such an expensive edition were left frustrated.

Jesus and the devil went through a sort of Bible drill. They didn't even need a written Bible. We know that Jesus had memorized the written Scriptures, but the devil also knows them and uses them for his own purposes.

Jesus rejected Satan's suggestion for satisfying His earthly appetite, referring to Deuteronomy 8:3, where Moses was preparing the children of Israel to enter the Promised Land after the forty years of wandering. Moses implored the people not to forget the times in the wilderness when God supplied them with manna. Jesus quoted Moses' words: "Man does not live on bread alone, but by every word that comes from the mouth of God."

Temptation and Rejection

Test one, passed.

So the lust-of-the-flesh strategy failed. Satan probably knew he'd better be at the top of his game. He took Jesus to the top of the Temple in Jerusalem … and quoted Scripture.

"Jesus, throw yourself off the top of this building, because God will command his angels concerning you, and they will lift you up in their hands, so that you will not strike your foot against stone."

Those words are from Psalm 91, a favorite chapter of both my wife and my mother. I was reading Psalm 91 to my mother when she passed away.

Satan does know Scripture, but he hates to have it quoted back at him. It would be good for us to know as much Scripture as possible so that we have a weapon against the wiles of the devil. In Ephesians 6, Paul wrote about the weapons God gives us to use in spiritual warfare. The Word of God is the *sword of the Spirit.*

Jesus swung that sword and quoted Deuteronomy 6:16: "Do not test the Lord your God as you did at Massah." *Massah* was the place where the children of Israel had questioned whether the Lord was still with them, and Moses was instructed to strike the rock for water. The name *Massah* means *test.*

Test two, passed.

Satan's next ploy was a strategy with which he's had great success, right up to this day. He attempted to trip up Jesus by appealing to His pride.

He took Jesus to a mountaintop and showed Him the kingdoms of the world.

"These are my kingdoms, all under my control. You can have them all if you'll only bow down and worship me."

Now how about that? Jesus could have bypassed the cross. He could have had the world He came to save. Couldn't He have done a lot of good by taking control of all those kingdoms?

Once again, Jesus quoted from Deuteronomy. (Jesus must have enjoyed Deuteronomy.) His response to Satan was Deuteronomy 6:13: "You shall worship the Lord your God and serve Him only."

Test three, passed.

Those years of study and memorization had served Jesus well. The devil left Him.

Could this grueling test have been necessary to help Jesus the man grow and mature? Was this intense struggle a preparation to strengthen Him for the mission ahead? The voice from Heaven at His baptism was a glorious affirmation. Was the victory over the temptations also a validation of His calling and mission?

Matthew reports that when the devil left Jesus, angels then came and took care of Him. What a wonderful outcome of this battle!

We tend to shy away from struggle and adversity. But could it be that God uses those hard places to confirm, strengthen, and enlarge our faith? Are times of what we would call testing actually times of preparation? Are angels waiting to minister to us as we come through the wilderness?

Luke adds the note that the devil left Jesus "until the next opportunity came" (Luke 4:13). The enemy of God was not going to give up targeting the human Jesus.

So when Jesus returned to His hometown and things turned ugly, even though the devil isn't mentioned specifically, we can guess that he had a hand in the events that transpired.

. . .

You've probably already noted that my hike on the Jesus Trail does not follow the chronological sequence of Jesus' life. We didn't start in Bethlehem. After Nazareth, I was going to Cana next, and then Capernaum, the hub of Jesus' ministry. And I wouldn't get to the Jordan River, site of Jesus' baptism, until a few days later.

We might as well just acknowledge here that reading the four Gospels and trying to sort out the chronological sequence of events in Jesus' ministry can be confusing. The writers of those accounts don't always seem to agree about *when* something happened or even about the details. Matthew, Mark, Luke, and John all wrote at different times, for different purposes. You'll remember that John said that it would take many books to spell out everything Jesus said and did. Each writer focused on scenes and messages he wanted to convey. The same thing happens when I write. Take my hike on the Appalachian Trail, for instance, and the resulting book, *Hiking Through.* I certainly didn't write about everything that happened, and I related some stories completely out of time sequence, depending on when it made the most sense to introduce them into the whole picture that was my story.

So as we walk through Israel together on the Jesus Trail, we'll reflect on places and events as Craig and I approached them, not necessarily as they happened in Jesus' lifetime.

. . .

One more word about Nazareth. And it's a rather sad scene to contemplate.

Jesus had completed his training to become a rabbi. He knew it was time to get the team together and get on with the mission. He'd been baptized, went on a fasting retreat, and came under the stiff attack from Satan.

After this, Jesus returned to Galilee and began preaching and teaching in various venues. Folks were quite impressed with what He had to say. That is, until He returned to His hometown and spoke in His own local synagogue.

It started out well enough.

Jesus might have been back in Nazareth to accompany His mother and family to a wedding in Cana. To my mind, it's more likely He wished to officially announce to His hometown who He was and what He was about.

Remember, Jesus had grown up with these people. I'm certain the town folks knew Him as a smart boy. He had studied to be a rabbi. He was the son of Joseph and Mary. They knew His brothers and sisters. They had all played together as children. They'd probably also heard that He had begun His teaching in Capernaum, by the Sea of Galilee.

While back home in Nazareth, He went to the synagogue, "as was His custom."

In my community, the Amish churches are divided into districts. Whenever a minister from a different district is visiting another church's service, he is invited to take part.

That's what happened to the young rabbi in Nazareth.

Imagine yourself in that scene.

You've grown up in a small town, known to everyone as so-and-so's son. Everyone knows you've been working toward a career out in the wider world; you studied a long time for it, and now you've done it. Your friends and neighbors were excited for you, sending you off with hearty wishes for a small-town kid to do well.

Yes, all those folks back home knew your dreams, but most people also knew that only a very few ever become famous politicians, movie stars, athletes, or televangelists. Let's be realistic, after all. You, however, *are* becoming quite famous and popular. The Internet is buzzing about your rising star.

You go back home for a visit. Wouldn't you expect to see the red carpet laid out, the band playing, and the mayor waiting to give you the key to the town? At the very least, there would be a reception, where everyone could drop in and congratulate you and maybe get your autograph. Or you might be recognized and welcomed and asked to say a few words at the service on Sunday morning in your home church.

Jesus was back home. He was invited to be a part of the church service. I imagine the small area was filled with locals, eager to hear what He might be teaching that day from the Torah.

Instead, He stood up and asked the young man in charge of the scrolls to bring Him the writings of Isaiah, the Old Testament prophet.

I'm not sure how the old scroll divided chapters, or if they even were divided into chapters and verses. In our modern Bibles, the Scripture Jesus read is the first two verses of Isaiah 61.

> The Spirit of the Lord is on me,
> because he has anointed me to preach good news
> to the poor.
> He has sent me to proclaim freedom for the prisoners
> and recovery of sight for the blind,
> to release the oppressed,
> to proclaim the year of the Lord's favor.

I can visualize it, and I can hear Jesus put the emphasis on the word *me.*

The custom was that the reader would sit down and invite dialogue about the reading just presented. But before Jesus sat down,

He made an astounding announcement.

"Today, this Scripture is fulfilled in your hearing."

It's about that time, I believe, that the town folks realized what had just happened.

"He didn't just say that, did he?" some might have asked the person next to them. "Did I hear that right?"

"Don't we know his mom and dad, his brothers and sisters? Didn't we see him grow up here in Nazareth? Now he's daring to suggest that he's the king we're promised!"

And we aren't told, but perhaps some folks whispered about his birth. "Wasn't his mother pregnant before she was married?"

The synagogue was buzzing. Surely no one that important could have come from Nazareth. How could this man they knew be making such outrageous claims?

And—imagine it—could Joseph and the rest of Jesus' family have been right there? In the midst of the outraged whispering? It's likely they were. They watched and listened as Jesus said these shocking things.

The Nazareth locals were going to put Jesus to the test.

"We heard you did healing in Capernaum. Let's see you do some healings here."

Jesus remarked that this town would not be in line for miracles. He reminded them of the time during a three-and-a-half-year drought when Elijah couldn't help even one Israeli person but was sent to a non-Jewish town to help a widow. There were many lepers in Israel during Elisha's time, but the only one he healed was Naaman, also a non-Jew. The lack of miracles was caused by a lack of faith, and Nazareth had no faith in Jesus.

Things unraveled quickly after that. Mob mentality set in. They were angry with this imposter, and ready to dispose of Him.

Can you imagine it all? Jesus comes home to spread His good news, and, instead, He gets death threats.

The mob forced Jesus out of the synagogue, all the way up the hill to the brow of Nazareth where they intended to throw Him off a cliff. But He slipped away and escaped.

They were neighbors, friends, childhood buddies, and probably even some family members—and they now turned against Him.

CHAPTER 9

The Miracles Begin

The next morning, we climbed a narrow, winding street in Old Nazareth. I say *climbed* because we walked *up* that street—literally—up 406 stone steps that led to the highest point in town. Could this have been the place where the mob tried to throw Jesus to His death? From the brow of the hill, we had a grand view of a vast valley below us, and far off in the distance, a town graced another hilltop.

We could see almost the entire stretch of our planned hike that day. Our destination was Cana, the town where Jesus performed His first miracle and set the local grapevine a-buzzing with rumors about Joseph and Mary's oldest son. Cana was only 13.4 kilometers (about 8.5 miles) from Nazareth. The walk would take us five hours, at the most.

Getting out of Nazareth wasn't as easy as imagined, though. The Jesus Trail is a work in progress; blazes are sometimes difficult to find, and detours and reroutes occur frequently. Portions of the trail run together with the Israel Trail, and if a hiker is not alert, it's easy to miss the point at which the two diverge. When a trail takes a turn, the blaze is curved in the direction to take.

On the brow of Nazareth, we searched in vain for a blaze with two white stripes separated by an orange one. After wandering aimlessly, searching for markers and finding none, we were forced to do something that is considered anathema to men: We looked at our map.

Finally moving forward, we had gone only a few hundred feet when the trail took us down over a steep hill and through a residential area.

I was stunned by what I saw. There were some attractive, newer houses, but trash littered the landscape. Folks apparently threw out refuse right beside their homes. Later, we would see frequent stretches along the highway where people drove by and randomly dumped all kinds of garbage.

My suspicion was that this was a cultural habit, but I wondered if a factor was also that many living in Arab towns believe they are living in occupied territory and therefore don't care. That may be a bit judgmental, however.

With the first mile under our belt, we were making good time heading toward Sepphoris. Then we realized we were already lost.

"Hey, Craig, have you seen any blazes lately?"

No, he hadn't.

We were walking through a broad valley, heading for who knows where. We could see Nazareth behind us, so we knew that at least we weren't in danger of wandering in the wilderness for several days.

After backtracking, we discovered an orange blaze painted on a stone, and we struck off in the right direction.

Soon after, we approached the hilltop where the ancient town of Sepphoris once stood. The town as Jesus knew it is no longer there. Now, we only see Sepphoris from the remains uncovered by archaeology. Excavations have already discovered beautiful mosaic floors, still intact, although the walls and roofs of buildings are gone. Herod's theater has been found—a 4,500-seat building. The city was apparently home to many rich and extravagant people. It was once called *the ornament of all Galilee.* The site is now Zippori National Park, and for a fee, visitors can wander through the excavations.

In Matthew 5, Jesus was teaching the Beatitudes to His disciples. He told them they were the light of the world, like a city on a hill that cannot be hidden. I wonder if He was recalling the sight of Sepphoris on its hill, not too far away from Nazareth as He was growing up.

. . .

The distance we would walk from Nazareth to Cana was 8.5 miles, a short hiking day. However, the pathway was a circuitous route, taking us through olive groves, over peaks, and down into valleys.

The olive trees of Israel are relatively short, not more than fifteen to twenty feet high. Trees often have two or more thick trunks, which are twisted and bent, sometimes at odd angles. Topped with a cloud of leaves that from a distance look fuzzy and soft, the trees seem to be a crowd of silver-haired, stooped ancients, who have lived to see centuries of life come and go.

The trail could be a simple path through groves and fields, but in sharp contrast, it at times followed rutted roads where people drove in to dump trash. This came as a shock to me, something I've never experienced before on a long-distance trail.

At the same time, the dumps provided some diversion along the way. On one small slope, a discarded tire lay along the path, just too tantalizing for me. With one quick flip, I sent it rolling down the hillside. Craig discovered something more practical—a case of overripe oranges that had been discarded. One orange looked as though it still retained some nourishment, and we shared it.

As we were treasure hunting in the dump, a young lady approached. She stopped, we had a brief discussion about the trail, and she told us she had taken a wrong turn and had to backtrack a considerable distance.

She also asked if we had picked up a paper describing reroutes for the following day. We did not realize such a paper existed. It didn't concern us, though, since as men we have a good sense of direction. (Or did we?) Of course, good sense of direction shouldn't be confused with good common sense, so I took a photo of her map. Just in case. As a last resort. It might be needed.

My photo of the map would be needed, but by the time it was time to resort to the last resort, it was too late.

. . .

A short distance before we arrived in Cana, we walked through another hilltop village known as Mash'had. In the Old Testament, this town was known as Gath Hepher. Jonah, the reluctant prophet, used to call this small burg home.

As we passed through town, I noticed houses built right by the main road with enclosures for animals attached directly to their living quarters. I could imagine that when Jesus was born in Bethlehem, the inn might have had a similar set up; although there was no room in the main house, the enclosure for the animals was immediately adjacent.

Mash'had is a Muslim town, and as luck would have it, the time for the call to prayer had arrived. Of course, since this happens five times a day, the chance of hearing it in any town one treks through is substantially increased. The minaret is the tallest structure in most towns, and the volume on the speakers is always turned way up. It's impossible to miss the call to prayer. The sounds blasting our hearing that day did not move our spirit to prayer at all. Indeed, my minister friend turned the prayer into a chant of his own.

"There are two Americans walking through your town. Please be advised, there are two Americans walking through your town." Craig pretended that was the message being relayed from the minaret tops warning the general populace of Jonah-land about the two Christian invaders in their streets.

In case that actually was the message, we hustled out of town.

Leaving Mash'had, we had a clear view of Cana, prominently displayed on yet another distant hilltop. Again we took the scenic route. The trail turned abruptly onto a rutted road that went downward and through an area littered with industrial building waste. This was *the Jesus Trail?* Did Jesus pass this kind of scene as He walked to a wedding in Cana one day?

Arriving in Cana, we looked for the Cana Wedding Guesthouse. I am certain that Jesus had better success in finding the location of the wedding to which He had been invited than we did in finding our lodging spot.

I put the address in my smart phone GPS, but that address baffled the wonderment that is an iPhone. Fortunately, I had a phone number for the guesthouse, and the young man who answered my call was in his car, driving on the very street we were following. Several twists and turns of a narrow alleyway brought us to the entrance of the Cana Wedding Guesthouse. We arrived just in time for the call to prayer.

When we inquired about a good eating spot for the evening meal, we were offered a home-cooked meal prepared by the proprietor's wife. A deal was struck, and we enjoyed a feast befitting two pilgrims in a foreign land.

Following our feast, we decided to stroll around town a bit. We passed the Franciscan Wedding Church along the way. It was built in 1879 over previous ruins. There is no way of knowing if this is the spot where Jesus performed His first miracle. As a matter of fact, even the exact location of the Cana of Jesus' time is in dispute, although it was certainly near the modern-day town. On our Israel trek, Craig often repeated "If not here, then near."

The Wedding Church in Cana claims to be built on the spot where Jesus performed His first miracle, but this, like so many places in Israel, may be only *near, if not here.* We do know that it is built over the ruins of at least one other church or synagogue. It's a beautiful stone building that includes a chapel where folks can renew their wedding vows and a museum with numerous artifacts, one of which is an ancient stone jar that supposedly was used at the wedding Jesus attended.

John recounted the event in his gospel. He wrote that this event was the first time Jesus "revealed His glory" (John 2:11), but apparently Jesus had already begun His teaching in Capernaum, because He went to the wedding with a number of people who were identified as disciples of the Teacher from Nazareth.

It would seem that this was a perfect opportunity to get started on miracles, but Jesus, at first, did not appear to be planning on this.

Let's join Jesus at the wedding and see what's happening.

. . .

These weddings could go on for several days. I know something of the preparation and planning that go into the one-day event that is an Amish wedding, so I can appreciate the work that must have been essential for a successful multi-day wedding celebration.

This wedding would have been a community event, and for a while, everything seemed to be going well.

But someone must have miscalculated. Perhaps more people had shown up than the hosts expected. Maybe when they invited Jesus, they had no idea He'd be bringing along some of His followers. I don't suppose RSVPs were common in those days.

Whatever the reason for the situation, the wait staff suddenly realized they were running out of wine. This would have been a great embarrassment for the hosts of the wedding.

Jesus' mother, Mary, was also in attendance that day. We don't know why, but she learned of the impending disaster. Then she went to Jesus and explained the problem.

For thirty years, Mary had been pondering, and I'm sure she often wondered when and how the prophecies about her son would be fulfilled.

Jesus' reply to Mary indicated that He did not think this was the time to perform a miracle. Maybe He was thinking that He would wait until returning to Capernaum. I find it fascinating that it was His mother who finally prompted Him to act.

Mary seemed to completely ignore Jesus' comment; she went to the servants and told them to do whatever He said. Moms apparently know things sons may not.

What changed Jesus' mind? Granted, He could have simply refused to do anything about the wine shortage. He had already given Mary His opinion. So He could have ignored the situation and His mother's expectation. However, to my mind, this might be a glimpse of His humanity. Perhaps, as a son, He wanted to respect His mother.

He gave the servants instructions: "Fill the water jars."

Don't you suppose the servants wondered what this man was planning to do? How could these jars of water help with their predicament of not having enough wine?

Furthermore, these jars were *not* to hold water for drinking. The six stone jars, probably from five to eight gallons in size, were intended to hold water for ceremonial washing. This water was used to thoroughly wash hands before eating, and it would also be used to clean dishes and cooking utensils, thereby rendering the jars unclean.

"Fill them to the brim." That left no room for any additional ingredients. Just water. Somehow that water turned into wine.

The servants did what they were told.

I like to imagine the moment when they realized what had happened. When did the water turn to wine? While it was still in the jars? When it was poured out? As they carried it to the tables? Did the servant who carried the first cup to the master of ceremonies know? Can you imagine the buzzing among the servants in the kitchen and those serving at the tables, as they whispered about what had happened?

The disciples with Jesus also knew what had happened, and it had an impact on them. At this point, it seems that they did not understand that this man was the Son of God. He was a man from Nazareth, a teacher teaching new things. But the miracle certainly convinced them that God was with their teacher.

And the wine was being served from unclean jars! That went against all the rules. It wouldn't be long, though, until everyone would be talking about this Teacher from Nazareth who claimed He had come to do away with rules and regulations that were constraining people.

You've got to love it! Jesus not only perplexed the religious Pharisees of the time, but He still perplexes modern-day Pharisee rule makers.

The Miracles Begin

Yes, let's dive right into the controversy.

Alcohol is a debated topic in many Christian churches. Some forbid it entirely; some are more tolerant on the matter.

I wrote a series of Amish novels in which Amish boys drank beer. At one book signing, an Amish lady picked up the book and happened to read that part of the story. She slammed the book down on the table and with righteous indignation informed me that Amish boys don't drink alcohol.

I wasn't aware one could stick one's head that deeply into sand. She put ostriches to shame.

I once heard a preacher twisting himself into knots as he tried to explain that what Jesus produced in those water jars was only grape juice. Jesus would never turn water into a sinful product, the preacher declared.

Since Jesus' first miracle was turning water into wine—and I do believe it was wine, not grape juice—I believe there's a message for us in the account. However, I also believe we are too often distracted from the rest of the story by our dogmatic beliefs on the consumption of beverages containing any degree of alcohol.

This question of what's sin and what isn't has troubled myself and many other barn-born Christians. We were taught that many *things* are sin. We were told of the evil influence of television, and as my young mind perceived the teachings, then whenever I saw a television set, that box in itself was sin. That may seem foolish, even incomprehensible, to many people, but that's the reality of growing up in a barn.

People did drink wine in Jesus' time. Jesus Himself drank it. However, Paul admonished people not to get drunk on wine. It leads to debauchery, he wrote in Ephesians 5. I'm sure folks who grew up with an alcoholic parent or people who have lost a loved one due to an alcohol-related accident can tell of the horrors of alcohol misused. Whether in Paul and Jesus' time or in ours, alcohol used in the wrong way brings terrible results. Yes, *sinful* results.

But a bottle of beer or wine can sit on your counter for years and it is not sin sitting there. You can take a bath in wine if you are so inclined, and you'll not be sinning. Jesus would never perform a miracle that created anything that was sinful. (You see, I've used the same argument to bolster my position that the grape-juice preacher used to prove his viewpoint.)

I'm not a proponent of drinking, and that's mostly a result of the way I was raised. In our household, wine and beer were not part of our diet because our church forbade it. But as an adult, responsible for my own decisions and choices, I choose not to partake, although yes, I have tasted.

I want to hasten to add that I'm also not a proponent of criticizing people who do choose to have wine with a meal.

Whether it's alcohol, television, the internet, anything … the *thing* is not sin. It's what people do with things that is sin. People are sinful; things are not. The difference might be obvious to you, but it took me a while to get this straightened out.

. . .

Later that evening, a group of us were gathered around a table on the veranda of the Wedding Guest House. Several of the guests had purchased small bottles of wine labeled as "Cana Wedding Wine." Capitalism at its best! When offered a taste, I humbly accepted.

It was horrible. I remarked that I'd appreciate a miracle from Jesus, turning that wine back into water.

CHAPTER 10

Contemplating and Ambulating

I have often wondered about that first miracle in Cana. The scene described by John in his account seems almost matter-of-fact. But no miracle can be matter-of-fact. What better time to contemplate the scene that day at the wedding than when I am right there (or near) where it happened?

I'm aware that the Bible warns us not to add anything to what's already been written in the Scriptures. I don't want to do that. I would never try to do that. I do, however, like to imagine the whys and wherefores and what ifs of events spoken of in Biblical accounts.

We born-in-a-barn Christians have heard so many of those stories so often that the significance of the details and the power of what Jesus was doing on earth is muted. We skim over the lines we read because we think, *I know all this.* Some of the accounts we can even recite in our sleep, like the familiar lines, *And it came to pass in those days, that there went out a decree from Caesar Augustus...*

Even the account of a man who was lied about, arrested, beaten, and then executed for something He did not do—for things *you and I did!*—does not move us at times.

John tells us in his book that it would take many additional books to contain all of the things Jesus did and taught. Mary had much on her mind, too. There were many things, beginning with the visit from the angel Gabriel, that Mary "pondered in her heart." Don't you suppose she often reflected on the words of the angel, Simeon, Anna, and the Old Testament prophets who had spoken of a coming Messiah? As she watched her son grow and mature both physically and spiritually, I'm sure she was also wondering how God was going to work out His plans—and just what part her son would play in those plans.

I was in Israel seeking to know Jesus better, so I was pondering, too. As I visited scenes from Jesus' life and ministry, I asked the Holy Spirit to reveal more to me about the truths of the Scriptures. I wanted to understand more fully what Jesus was like as a man and what He had lowered Himself to do so that I could live forever.

Here, in Israel, I wanted to find a deeper connection to the man I claim to follow. One way to do that, I hoped, was to place myself in the scenes described in the Gospels, learning more about details of His life and the culture in which He lived.

I wanted to know Jesus better.

. . .

The next morning, we were going in the wrong direction but were making good time. The goal for the day's end was the base of Mt. Arbel. If everything went according to plan, I would soon have a glimpse of the Sea of Galilee in the distance.

Our guidebook promised a McDonald's at a road intersection

named Golani Junction. McDonald's coffee and a breakfast sandwich—I could taste it already. We would certainly be there in time for breakfast, since we had been awakened at 4:30 a.m. by a voice from on high calling us to prayer and telling us (in Arabic, of course) *Prayer is better than sleep.*

The usual mounds of rubbish littered our pathway. We even passed couches and chairs that had been dumped hither and yon.

Occasionally we walked through olive groves where ripening olives awaited harvest.

Our map showed that the trail ran parallel to the highway, then veered off and skirted a military area. I saw a highway off in the distance, an intersection, and a gas station. But we searched in vain for the yellow sign suggesting breakfast. We crossed the highway for a closer look. No McDonald's.

We did, however, see a café nearby, and we availed ourselves of a good breakfast there.

We had left the Jesus Trail as we chased breakfast. Following the trail around the military area would have brought us to Golani Junction and the promised fast-food breakfast, but we'd taken a wrong turn. If we had looked at my photo of the updated map the lady showed us the day before, we might have corrected our error. But who needs maps when one can see and perceive?

So although we *saw* there was no McDonald's, we *perceived* the situation incorrectly. We didn't realize we were at the wrong intersection.

Which means that after breakfast, we kept on walking—with our minds still in the grip of misconceptions.

We knew that to get to our destination for the day, we would pass through Kibbutz Lavi, a place Craig had stayed during a previous visit to Galilee.

The 13th Disciple

Off in the distance, a series of buildings protruded from the top of a mountain. Craig asked a young man if those buildings were Kibbutz Lavi. The young man couldn't speak or understand English, so the easiest way to get rid of us was to shake his head yes. That affirmation was enough to send us on our merry way, still traveling under wrong perceptions.

We did give a quick perusal to the map then—perhaps a little too quick—and determined that if we continued to walk along the olive groves lining the highway, we would eventually intersect with the Jesus Trail and again be back on course.

That intersection never occurred, but we stubbornly plodded on.

At one point, we seemed to have reached an impasse. An embankment with a chain link fence barred our way and caused us some hesitation, but we found a low point and leaped over the fence to soldier on.

No orange blazes appeared. It seemed impossible that we weren't locating the trail. At last, a major intersection presented itself. At this intersection, one road led upward toward the hilltop buildings of our assumed destination, and we turned onto that road and were once again back on the Jesus Trail (again, assumed). No signs or blazes confirmed that, but who needs signage when you've seen the destination with your own two eyes?

We kept walking. Lining the road now were groves where folks were picking olives.

What we ignorant Americans didn't know was that the intersection we had just stumbled on was the Golani Junction. When we took that left turn up the hill, we had just missed the McDonald's we had searched for earlier. Had we been about one hundred feet higher, we could have seen the sign.

A lifeline was tossed our way. We had just started our plod uphill when a car stopped and the driver inquired if we wanted a ride.

If only we had mentioned that we were walking to Kibbutz Lavi! Then the driver could have had a good laugh and told us we were going the wrong way and we could have corrected our directional error. But we foolishly thought we were in no need of aid and said no thanks, we were fine, we preferred to walk.

Isn't that what we often do in our personal lives? Convinced we are right, we go marching off in the wrong direction. God sends a messenger to inform us of the error of our way, but we're too proud or arrogant to accept help.

The buildings we had seen from afar slowly took on the definition of housing units. Craig peered at the landscape. Yes, indeed, he thought he recognized those buildings. There should be an entrance just up ahead, he said.

Of course, it only makes sense that any series of buildings would have ingress and egress somewhere; and in time, an entrance did appear, confirming our belief that we were where we needed to be.

Craig remembered two landmarks from Kibbutz Lavi: a roundabout and a business that makes synagogue furniture. Good, there was the roundabout. Craig thought he recognized a building that looked like a factory. Apparently when one is blissfully unaware that one is lost, everything can be imagined to look familiar.

In reality, we had arrived at an intersection known as Zomet Netofa. We were headed northward toward the Golan Heights. The development we had stumbled upon was a residential area in a small farming community. Farm fields stretched out toward the horizon.

Craig finally admitted, though, that things just weren't making sense.

A young boy on a bicycle approached us. He spoke broken English.

"Is this the Kibbutz Lavi?"

"Har Nimra," he replied. At that time, we had no idea what those words meant.

I guessed the young boy—or should I say, *the young gentleman,* since he was very professional and kind—to be about ten years old. He was delivering papers, but he took the time to help us.

"Follow me to my house," he said. "My family is at home. They will help you."

We followed, and without so much as informing his parents that they had company, he invited us into the house, scampered upstairs, and returned with his mom. Soon his dad also joined us, along with an older son.

When we explained our dilemma, we were informed just how far off the path we had strayed.

This was not Kibbutz Lavi. This was a residential area with a wide mix of people. The gentleman we were talking to was an engineer. While we conversed with the family, the young boy who had rescued us returned with apples and water for us. The elder son was home on leave from the military and agreed to take us back to Kibbutz Lavi. We offered to pay him for the inconvenience if he would drive us there.

We zoomed back down the mountain and soon reached the intersection where we had made the wrong turn at the Golani Junction. And now we saw it—that yellow McDonald's sign.

Finally back on the right road, we soon reached Kibbutz Lavi, and I saw the actual furniture building and everything else Craig had so carefully described to me.

We thanked our driver and handed him money. He shook his head vigorously and refused to take any payment.

That was the first of many acts of kindness shown to us by Jewish people. We would learn the importance they place on doing good deeds for others. For Jews, rescuing strangers in distress (like us) or otherwise helping others is a commandment from God, known as a *mitzvah*. No payment is needed or desired. Jews feel it's actually a "God connection" for them. We sometimes hear folks talk about an event as a "Jesus thing," an event that has no explanation other than that Jesus has a meaning or purpose for us in the happening. This Jewish family who welcomed us into their house would believe similarly that it was a God event that brought us to them. For Craig and me, it certainly was a Jesus thing!

In our busy lives, I wonder how often we are presented with an opportunity to observe mitzvah by helping a friend or a stranger. We too often think *What's in it for me?* instead of *What does God ask of us?*

. . .

From the beginning of its history, Jerusalem has been a desired and contested city. Long before David conquered it and it became known as "the City of David," surrounding nations had fought over and gained and lost control of Jerusalem. Its history has repeated that pattern after David, right up to this very day.

By the year 1095, Jerusalem had been under Muslim control for nearly five hundred years. In autumn of that year, Pope Urban II issued a decree that an army force be assembled to return Jerusalem to Christian control. The march would eventually be known as the First Crusade, because more wars between Catholic and Islam forces were to come.

That first military campaign was a success, and Jerusalem was retaken by Christian forces.

In 1144, Muslims captured a town in Turkey, which had been

founded as a result of the First Crusade. A second decree came from Pope Eugene III, and European kings again aligned to fight the Muslim forces; but this time, the Muslims were victorious.

There would be nine crusades in all, continuing from 1095 to 1291, as allied European Christian armies fought the followers of Muhammad for control of areas of the Holy Land, including Jerusalem.

Today, you'll hear our society's liberal elements and Islam sympathizers flinging accusations that Christians slaughtered Muslims during the crusades. The reality was that Muslims had captured two thirds of the old Christian world and were prepared to convert the entire world to Islam by force. If the Christian world didn't fight back, Islam would be the world's only religion. The reality was that both sides were guilty of slaughter.

Not much has changed. Islam still holds the vision of someday controlling the world.

What's the point of all this history?

One of my intentions is to remind us how fortunate we are in this country to have the freedom and protection to live and worship in whatever way we choose.

Another reason for the brief history lesson is that as we left Kibbutz Lavi, I was about to walk over history.

. . .

We were crossing a vast, open field. Ahead loomed a steep hill known as the Horns of Hattin. This is an extinct volcano with a flat area—the crater—at the center of two peaks that look like the horns of a bull.

The Jesus Trail led up and over the two horns and the flat plateau between them. Some traditions say that this is the location of Jesus' Sermon on the Mount. The hills rising above the flat area make it easy to imagine the scene with Jesus teaching from a hillside to a crowd of people, but, like so many other sites in Israel, there is no way to be certain of this. In fact, a stronger tradition sets Jesus' famous sermon on another mountain, now called *the Mount of Beatitudes*. The Church of the Beatitudes has been built on that mountain.

During the Second Crusade, a Muslim army leader named Saladin fought the army of the Crusaders at the Horns of Hattin in a decisive battle on July 4, 1187. The Crusader army had left Sepphoris and was marching through the area in an effort to reach Tiberius, which was under Muslim siege, but they had miscalculated and their army was blocked off from any water source. Saladin set fires all around the area, and the resulting smoke made it even more difficult for the parched knights to hold their ground and fight. The Crusaders were soundly defeated on the Horns of Hattin, and subsequently the Muslim army retook much of the Holy Land, including Jerusalem.

Two years later, the Third Crusade began. Doesn't it seem as if we are now in something like the Ninety-ninth Crusade against followers of Muhammad?

Atop the Horns of Hattin, we were blessed with a gorgeous view in all directions. Below us lay extensive farmlands and Moshav Arbel. A *moshav* is a collective of farmers. It is similar in nature to a Jewish *kibbutz*.

We were headed to Arbel, a town at the foot of the towering Mt. Arbel. That mountain is just northeast of the Horns of Hattin, and it is a third place where some have speculated that Jesus delivered His most famous sermon.

We also had our first glimpse of the Sea of Galilee, far off in the distance. The Sea of Galilee is actually a lake, and it has three names used in Biblical accounts. Some folks might think Jesus was walking around three separate seas, but the *Sea of Gennesaret,* the *Sea of Tiberius,* and the *Sea of Galilee* all refer to the same body of water. In Hebrew today, the lake is also referred to as *Lake Kinneret.*

It seemed impossible that on the following day I would actually be walking along the shore of that famous sea.

CHAPTER 11

The 13ᵗʰ Disciple

From the peak of Mt. Arbel, at 1,250 feet, we had a panoramic view over the entire Sea of Galilee and the surrounding area. This was the countryside in which Jesus carried out much of His ministry. I scanned the view and attempted to comprehend what had taken place below me during those three years when Jesus walked the landscape. Craig read a passage of Scripture and prayed, and we spent several minutes in contemplative silence.

Directly west of Mt. Arbel lies a sister mountain, Mt. Nitai. In the valley between them is the small village of Wadi Hamam. *Wadi* is the word for *ravine* or *valley.* Rainy periods turn this area into a bog, making hiking difficult. A spring with good drinking water flows freely there as well.

The two sister mountains were originally one mountain. An earthquake split them apart. This reminded me of the prophecy in Zechariah 14:4 that foresees Jesus standing one day on the Mount of Olives and that mountain also splitting in half, forming a great valley.

The 13ᵗʰ Disciple

That prophecy seems more understandable now that I know something about the tectonic plates along the Jordan Rift Valley, a geological depression that has its beginnings at the source of the Jordan River by Mt. Hermon, includes all of the Jordan River Valley, and extends to the Red Sea. It is a fault line similar to the one in California known as the San Andreas Fault. All that is necessary is a command from the Lord, and the crust of the earth will pull apart.

In a few days, I expected to be standing atop the Mount of Olives. One of the things I would try to visualize is what the Mount might look like someday when that split occurs.

From our vantage point in the sky, we also saw lush farmlands spread below us. Directly north of Mt. Arbel is the village of Migdal, the modern name of Magdala, home of Mary Magdalene. Farther to the northeast, along the shore of the Sea of Galilee, was Capernaum; and beyond that city lay Bethsaida, the home of Peter and Andrew.

Most of these towns encircling the Sea of Galilee have names linked to the fishing trade. When Jesus arrived in Capernaum to set up His ministry, He came to an area where catching and selling fish was the main source of income. The word *magdala* means tower; it is believed that some type of tower structure was used there to dry fish. The literal meaning of *Bethsaida* is *fishing village*. The folks readily available to become Jesus' disciples were fishermen.

With that glorious preview to the next few days, we descended Mt. Arbel. A hiker has two options when leaving that peak. The easier route is more circuitous; the more difficult path goes down the face of the cliff. The latter route has handholds embedded in the rocks, similar to ladder rungs. The trail is closed in wet weather, and anyone who has any queasiness about heights is advised not to use this path.

One need hardly guess which route we took.

The 13ᵗʰ Disciple

Our climb downward took us past numerous caves in the cliffs of Mt. Arbel. Over the centuries, these have been used as dwellings or fortresses for different groups of people. Jews who were hiding out from King Herod took refuge in these caves. Access paths were steep and narrow, hardly suitable for Herod to send troops upward. Eventually he devised a basket-like apparatus with which he lowered his soldiers down over the cliff to either pull out the cave dwellers and throw them to their deaths or to toss fire into the hideouts and burn to death anyone who refused to come out.

. . .

When we reached the foot of Mt. Arbel, we could smell the sea before we could see it.

One of the things I enjoy about long-distance hiking is the diversity of landscapes through which one walks. On my Appalachian Trail hike, I followed a path that went mainly through woods and up over mountains, and I enjoyed the beauty of nature at its best. Beautiful wildflowers bloomed profusely along the trail. Many waterfalls refreshed the soul. Every mountaintop offered a scenic view for the weary traveler. When I hiked across Spain on the Camino de Santiago, I marveled at the ancient towns, the ornate cathedrals with their beautiful stained glass windows, and, of course, the feasts of local food presented along the way.

The main attraction of any hike is the pathway itself and what it allows one to see. The rocky Appalachian Trail often meant I had to walk with my head down, watching every precarious step. A person is always one step away from disaster on that hike.

Now, Israel was presenting a landscape completely unlike anything I'd experienced before. That in itself added excitement to every day. I marveled again that I was there, my feet perhaps stirring up some of the same dust that Jesus' feet had stirred.

Instead of dust, though, we were slogging through a bit of Wadi Hamam muck. At the edge of town, we crossed a stream and followed it a distance through more mucky areas, where horses were doing their best to stay on solid ground.

Next, we entered an olive grove. The branches had endured an extreme pruning, but where each branch had been pruned back, three other branches were growing out of the stump.

Pruning is essential for new growth. I'm sure many of my readers could relate how God has pruned them in their own lives. It's not a pleasant thing to endure, but invariably it does lead to a better understanding of God's plan for one's life. That is, if we endure the trial.

According to the map, the Jesus Trail and the Israel Trail had been running together and supposedly were going to split near where we were hiking among olive and banana trees. However, we were probably the ones who needed to split—from the trail we were following. We hiked along a banana grove, followed a trail through a tunnel of wild plants and weeds, and emerged from the tunnel, admitting once again that we had no idea where we were or if we were headed toward the Sea of Galilee or westward toward the Mediterranean.

Once out of the banana fields, we stumbled onto a major highway. My fearless hiking partner, having been to the area before, remembered a gas station where he had eaten the best falafels of his lifetime. We should eat there, was his suggestion. This would be one of those adventures in local eating, I thought, so of course I agreed. I'd never had a falafel, though, and had no idea what they were.

I'll have a tank of gas, an oil change, clean the windows, and, oh yes, one falafel to go.

Off we struck, looking for the gas station. Again going in the wrong direction.

"Everything has changed," he lamented. It seemed the old gas station had been torn down and replaced by a new building. We did find a café that offered falafels, but Craig said they were not nearly the quality that he remembered having at the old gas station.

We resumed our quest to get back on the Jesus Trail and hiked on down the road.

Before too long, Craig yelled, "There it is! *That's* the gas station where they serve those great falafels!"

We stopped in and found a small area in the front where falafels were indeed being served to travelers with a better sense of direction than us.

A short road walk followed, and much to our relief, we discovered a trail marker where both the Jesus Trail and the Israel Trail led toward the Sea of Galilee. The rediscovered trail led through some underbrush, and at last we reached the shores of the famous sea.

We were in an area known as Ginosar.

The Sea of Galilee, with a pebbly and sandy beach, looked like any other lake. Off to our right (the southeast) and a few miles away, we could see the town of Tiberius sprawled up a hillside. Other than that, not much commercialism was visible. That amazed me; in America, resort areas crowd along sandy beaches or cluster around famous spots.

We also saw no sign of possible overnight accommodations. Perhaps we would finally need those tents we had brought along as a backup plan in case we were one day without a comfortable bed for the night.

As we walked north, the beach widened out and became sandier. A group of people waded at the edge of the water, and children ran and played on the sand. These folks seemed to have come from an edifice set back some distance from the beach.

Our hopes rose.

Indeed, it was a lodging spot known as the Karei Deshe Guest House. A beautiful inner courtyard was filled with palm trees and plants. The facility had sixty rooms and was considered a youth hostel. We discovered that many of the rooms had been booked by an extended Jewish family celebrating Shabbat together.

A restaurant serving kosher meals was also on site. For a modest fee, we had a nice room; and for a few shekels more, we could join the approximately one hundred Jewish folks gathered there for the evening meal. Breakfast was also included.

Supper was still an hour away, so I strolled out to the seashore to watch the sun set. The beach was abandoned, and I positioned a chair close to where the ripples were washing against the shore.

Off to my right, Tiberius soaked in the remains of the twilight. Offshore, lights blinked from distant boats. As daylight faded and the sun slipped below the horizon behind me, I closed my eyes in silent reverie.

It was the time of day known as the gloaming, that time between light and darkness. For me, this is often a time of introspection. Something about the lengthening of shadows and the approach of twilight often turns me a bit melancholy. Morning is the time for expectation of achievements. The time to work, as the Bible says, is while it's still day. But when the hour comes that signifies another day has passed, I often wonder, *Did I get anything accomplished?*

I closed my eyes, to contemplate the answer to that question. I had climbed a mountain, hiked through olive groves, walked along and through banana fields, fought through briars and brambles, and finally arrived at the Sea of Galilee.

Slowly my body relaxed, and my mind eased into a state of total peace. Did I fall asleep, did I dream, or did it really happen?

. . .

Although the light was waning, I recognized the figure walking toward me. It was the teacher from Capernaum. I also knew what He was doing there on the shore. He was looking for disciples.

I waved. *Over here!*

One would have thought that I'd have jumped up from the chair and rushed toward Him. Since this was my dream or imagination, I didn't.

"Grab a chair, my friend," I offered. "Should I wash your feet? Plenty of water available here."

Well, what would you have said, meeting Jesus for the first time? I was understandably a bit nervous.

"So, Jesus, I hear you're picking disciples to assist you in your ministry. I'm available. I want to be your disciple."

"Glad to hear that," He replied. "I always welcome more help. I already have The Twelve chosen, but I do have another group who is working on logistics, helping to procure lodging and supplies for the ministry. We're growing fast, and seventy-two people are working on those details. You could be Number 73."

I realize this is a reversal of the accounts we read of Jesus calling His disciples. Usually He is the one to give the invitation. Now I was initiating the process … But, hey, remember? It's my imagination. And furthermore, we don't know how those seventy-two came to be associated with the ministry. Perhaps *they* were volunteers.

"I'd actually prefer to be your 13th disciple, if you don't mind. I'm sure You know that I've been seeking for years to understand exactly what it means to follow You. I want to do it. And I want to do it right, so I'm ready and willing to learn."

"Being a disciple isn't an easy way of life, Paul. Sometimes we don't even know where we will eat or sleep. And the church leaders and the legal folks don't like us at all."

"I know all about that," I replied. "I'm from the future, you know. I already know about the traps being set for you. I can help you avoid some of those. Just imagine how helpful I could be."

"Are you suggesting *I* don't already know all about that?" asked Jesus. Was He smiling just a bit?

Of course. I should have thought before opening my mouth.

"Here is my suggestion for you, my dear seaside sitter," He went on. "Go back home and be my 13th disciple there. Tell folks you meet that they are all to be my disciples. Write about it. Change the world, one life at a time."

"Write about it? So you know about me and what I'm doing now?"

"Since you were formed in your mother's womb."

"Then you know that I've traveled the world over, trying to discover how to truly follow you. It seems so difficult to understand at times."

"My yoke is easy; my burden is light."

It was so easy to be comfortable with Him, and I was audacious enough to rib Him a bit.

"You're just quoting Scripture to me now."

At that, He did laugh aloud.

"It's all there, Paul, in the Scriptures. Seek and you will find, knock and the door will be opened to you."

"Is that the NIV or the King James you're quoting?"

He laughed again as He slipped away in the growing darkness.

The 13th Disciple

"Hey, Jesus, I'll be in Jerusalem in a few days," I called after Him. "Perhaps I can join you for supper?"

. . .

The ringing of a dinner bell reminded me it was indeed suppertime, and it startled me back to reality. Or did it startle me from reality?

There was a good reason the beach was empty except for me and Jesus. And He wasn't *supposed* to be there; He surely knew the error He was making, being out that late on the Sabbath. Yet He had stopped to talk with me. Of course, He was always a bit of a rule breaker.

It was Friday, *Shabbat* for Jews. A day of rest. This would be similar to Christians observing Sunday as a day of rest.

Throughout the day, we had heard people greeting one another with *Shabbat Shalom. Shalom* means *peace.* They were wishing each other a peaceful day of rest.

About midafternoon, workers cease working to prepare for Shabbat. Many will make a trip to the market to prepare for a family meal together.

Shabbat typically starts eighteen minutes before sunset and ends the following evening at sunset. So, from Friday evening to Saturday evening is the Sabbath Day for the Jewish people.

Shabbat starts with a candle-lighting ceremony. The ladies light the candles, although if a woman is not present, a man may do it. A single lady will light one candle; a married lady will light two, plus, if desired, one additional candle for each child. A blessing is spoken over the children as part of the candle-lighting ceremony. The meal follows the candle lighting and blessing.

The 13ᵗʰ Disciple

We were not invited to the candle ceremonies, but we were invited to the feast.

And what a feast it was. It was the first meal I've ever had that had been prepared and blessed according to Jewish rituals.

A buffet offered a wide variety of fruits and vegetables, olives, hummus, and a number of dipping sauces. Next came salmon, chicken, beef, roasted potatoes, string beans, rice, and more. A separate table held soups and breads. The dessert table displayed chocolate mousse, a variety of tarts, and a plethora of other delectable delights.

During the meal, I was amazed at the interaction of the family. Many of us are so busy with our own lives, that it's all we can do to keep track of our immediate family. This extended family of about one hundred and at least three generations meets at that establishment several times a year to celebrate Shabbat together.

I believe that one of the factors making the Jewish people such a powerful entity in the world is the cohesiveness of family. That is what makes communities and countries strong. The devil realizes this; he's working hard to destroy the structure of *family* in America.

Recently I was going through my grandfather's writings. My grandfather was an Old Order Amish man and unique in his day, in that he was a gifted writer and singer and had an overwhelming passion to reach lost souls. (The Amish community is not known as being overly mission-minded when it comes to the outside world.) He was also a man of intense prayer.

My grandfather had ten children; my father was the youngest of the ten. Dad recently passed away, at a youthful age of ninety-one. We as a family sure hated to see him go that young. Two other brothers had gone before him, at ages ninety-two and one hundred. My one remaining uncle is still very alert at age ninety-six.

The 13th Disciple

Here is what my grandfather wrote about his ten children:

I do believe not one of my children will dare to meet me before the "Tribunal of Christ" in an unprepared or unregenerated state, because I have continually pointed out to them "The Way to God" and the "Way of Life" by example, precept, and prayer. None of them is excusable.

He ended his thoughts that day with this reminder: *Remember, each one of us must give an account of himself to God.*

I am confident that my grandfather's prayers for his family were answered. I saw the results in the homes of my uncles and aunts. The love of God shone through all of those abodes.

My parents knew and trusted that whenever I was in an uncle or aunt's home, I would get the same training and needed discipline that I received at my parents' house. Seeing the interaction of this large Jewish family made me realize again how fortunate I had been to grow up in such a Christian environment.

I also know that such an environment doesn't "just happen." It is created by effort on the part of family members. My grandfather led by the example of his daily walk, showing his family what it meant to be a Christian family man with an intense, genuine prayer life.

My dad, likewise, desired and prayed for the same things for me and my four siblings. He had been taught by his father, and in turn, taught his children. From the moment each one of us was born, Mom and Dad prayed for our salvation. That praying never stopped until they took their last breaths.

My mother passed away one week after my dad. With all five of her children gathered round her during her last moments on earth, I asked her if she had any final words or instructions for us.

"Yes," she answered, "make sure all of you meet me in Heaven someday."

I am confident that Mom and Dad's prayer, like my grandfather's, will be honored and answered.

Parents, we have a great responsibility to make certain our children know the way and the truth. Those lives that have been entrusted to us are so precious. Everyone has an eternal soul that will live on beyond this earthly life. Where each spends that eternity is largely dependent on a parent's prayer life and the example they set.

CHAPTER 12

Choosing Disciples

The first rays of dawn found me on the shores of the Sea of Galilee again, seated at the same place as the previous evening. I had gone out to the shore while it was still dark. I've always thought it would be special to sit and watch the sun rise over this famous water. I wonder if Jesus got up early in the morning during His time here. I'm sure He enjoyed a beautiful sunrise or sunset as much as I do.

Slowly, the sea and its boundaries became more visible. I was facing the east side of the lake. Across from me, a glimmer of light broke the grayness as the sun peeked over the opposite hilltops.

Seven miles across the water is an area known as the Decapolis, ten cities founded by the soldiers of Alexander the Great. Like so many other conquerors who wanted to shape the world, Alexander was determined to Hellenize all of his conquests; that is, to spread the Greek culture across all of his kingdom. And like so many other areas, the towns of the Decapolis have been fought over and ruled by many different armies, including the Greeks, Romans, and Muslims.

The 13th Disciple

In Jesus' time, that area across the Sea of Galilee was off limits to Jews. A "good" Jew would never set foot there. That culture was far from the Jewish way of life. We know, though, that Jesus went there at least twice in His ministry.

There is some thought that when the prodigal son left for the "far country," he ended up across the Sea of Galilee in one of those ten towns. Can you imagine his father, looking across the sea to the eastern shore, suspecting that is where his son went, longing to go search for him—but knowing he could not?

On one of the hilltops across from where I was sitting, archaeologists have unearthed the remains of an old village known as Hippos, one of the towns of Decapolis. This was the region of the Gerasenes, mentioned in the Gospel of Mark, chapter 5. It's near where Jesus drove the demons out of the man roaming about the cemetery. You remember him: he was the wild man who lived in the burial caves, howling and cutting himself. The townsfolk had tried locking him up, but he had a supernatural strength and broke any restraints they had used. I can imagine that everyone thought he was a hopeless case, and just gave him a wide berth.

We've all heard or read Mark's account. But there are events in that story that compel me to contemplate.

I wonder what the disciples thought when Jesus told them to get in the boats and go to the other side (chapter 4 of Mark). They'd probably never ventured there before. But Mark also wrote that other boats followed.

Whatever the disciples thought, Jesus took that boat ride for one reason: one man. There was a demon-possessed man on the other side of the lake who needed the help of someone with authority.

During that boat ride, a vicious storm hit. Waves crashed and washed over the side of the boat, which was very nearly capsizing. I can imagine their fear; I was in a similar situation on my kayak trip down the Mississippi. I was at the mercy of the elements. Immense water, strong winds, a flimsy craft—we humans are no match for such storms.

Jesus had had a busy, exhausting day. The crowds had worn Him out. He was relaxing and had dozed off, peacefully asleep.

I wonder if the devil realized he was in danger of losing a whole contingent of demons he had living in a man? Did he bring that storm, hoping to turn back the boats or capsize them? I'm sure Satan was getting quite concerned at this point. Every effort he had made to intercept the coming of the Messiah had failed. Now this teacher from Nazareth was even casting out evil spirits. I can just imagine the devil watching events unfold and becoming increasingly frustrated as he was thwarted at every turn. When Satan saw Jesus heading across the Sea of Galilee to the opposite shore where no self-respecting Jew would set foot, he knew something was afoot.

And Jesus seemed to be heading right for the spot where the devil had a legion of demons residing. Something must be done. Could it be that as prince and power of the air, Satan caused that big storm, hoping Jesus would never reach that far shore?

Satan should have known, though. He should have seen the pattern that was being established. Satan would always lose when Jesus was involved. Fortunately, that still holds true for us today.

But maybe Satan was aiming again at the humanity of Jesus? Of course the other men in the boat were terrified; maybe Satan thought he could intimidate the human Jesus.

My thoughts were interrupted by a most beautiful sight. The brilliant sun was now fully above the horizon, and the entire sea was aglow with golden morning light. This was the scene that Jesus and the disciples and all the folks in this fishing village would have witnessed each day as they began their day's activities.

By this day's end, I myself would go to the far country on the opposite seashore. Instead of taking a boat, I would traverse the entire way on foot and by hitching a ride. What I did not know was what an amazing journey I would have.

. . .

We were headed to Capernaum, on the north shore of the Sea of Galilee, and we had no idea where eventide might find us.

Our first stop that morning was in an area known as Tabgha. The meaning of *Tabgha* is *seven springs*. Here, seven freshwater springs flowed from the hillsides into the sea. Some of these springs fed warm water into the sea, and this made the fishing grounds in this area especially promising. With freshwater readily available, this was also a good location for fishermen to clean their nets and boats and, possibly, also clean up their own stinky fish aroma before heading home for the evening.

It is believed that this area of seven springs is where Jesus might have picked His first disciples.

Capernaum was just around the corner from Tabgha, so Jesus would have had only a short walk to this area that drew the fishermen. As He approached one day, He saw Simon and his brother Andrew casting a net into the water. It took skill and strength to cast the nets outward and let them unfurl so they would settle properly into the water. This fishing was much more strenuous than casting a fly.

"Hey, guys, how about a job change?"

That's not how Mark describes the conversation, but it certainly is what Jesus meant.

"How about giving up fishing for fish and joining me in fishing for people?"

Choosing Disciples

I've often wondered why Jesus chose fishermen to be His disciples. Now I realize that this was a fishing village, and that is who was available.

In another area with other predominant occupations, how would Jesus' ministry have been different? Would His parables have changed?

How about your occupation, dear reader? Could you give it up? Some do. *Join me,* Jesus might say. *Let's go nursing for people.* Mother Teresa answered that call. How about lawyers, teachers, carpenters? Could you leave what you are doing for yourself and do it for Jesus? Of course, for many folks with debt and children and obligations, it might not be possible. Or is it? Certainly, it's easier for some than others.

Above all, saying yes to Jesus' invitation to follow Him is a leap of faith. That's a cliché, I know. But it *is* a leap—a gigantic change. We leave what we are doing for our own goals and desires, and we join up with Him in His mission. And it's a change made *only* by faith. It's only our faith that assures us that where He will lead us is where we truly want and need to be going. I confess that in my own life, it has often seemed that He leads down paths that I would prefer not to follow. But my faith keeps me following, even though my feet are sometimes dragging.

I was feeding people food for their bodies in my restaurant, working toward my own goals (which, I would offer humbly, were good, sensible, practical goals), when Jesus wondered if I would be willing, instead, to feed people with written words. Yes, it was a huge leap of faith for me.

I have now in my travels met many people who have taken this leap of faith. They seem to have several characteristics in common. For the most part, they are contented and happy. Certainly, in many cases, they do not have as much money as they might have had, but what price can one put on contentment?

. . .

Tradition says that Tabgha is also the site of the hillside all-you-can-eat fish story.

All four Gospels give the account. Jesus had just received the message that his cousin, John the Baptist, had been beheaded. He wanted to get away, find a solitary place along the sea somewhere. I imagine He wanted time to reflect on His cousin's brutal death.

Jesus also had twelve elated disciples who probably wanted time to talk with Him about everything that they had experienced. He had sent them out to preach and heal in surrounding communities, and they had just returned and had amazing things to report.

Jesus and His disciples got into a boat, but folks discovered where He was headed, word spread quickly, and people ran along the shore to meet Him. As soon as He stepped off the boat, He was surrounded by people asking to be healed.

This commotion went on all day. Imagine yourself as one of Jesus' disciples. Even with all the excitement of what's happening, weariness starts to set in. The stream of people who want to see Jesus is endless. Some of them are pushy, even rude. You and the other disciples and Jesus can't even take a few minutes of peace in which to eat. You can see Jesus is tired, and you're exhausted yourself. It's been a busy day, and some of these people are beginning to wear on your patience. It's not unrealistic to speculate that some normal human tendencies must have been surfacing as the day wore on—hunger and weariness bringing on grouchiness, impatience, and maybe even short tempers.

As long as we're contemplating the humanity of this scene, let's step back a moment and think about those twelve disciples who have just returned from visiting other towns. Jesus had sent them out in twos and had instructed them to tell people that the Kingdom of God had come. He also gave them the authority to heal and to cast out demons.

Can you imagine? They were given the power to heal diseases and to defeat Satan's demons. Those men whose resumes showed only "Fisherman." He sent greedy, shrewd Judas. Thomas, who we've dubbed a doubter. Peter, the impulsive one. Matthew, considered "scum" by many Jews because of who he used to be. Those ordinary, flawed people were given extra-ordinary powers as Jesus' disciples.

Yet we see them struggling to understand and believe throughout Jesus' time with them. Sometimes we think, *Why don't they get it? They have witnessed everything Jesus said and did, but they still don't believe?*

Why don't we get it? We have these accounts of Jesus' ministry and miracles from eyewitnesses. We have His words to us. We know He is alive. We have seen how Jesus can change lives in our own times. And we have God's Word about both the end of our own lives and the end of the story of humanity.

And yet, we struggle to have faith enough to put our trust in His leading. We protest that we are too uneducated, doubtful, untrained, impulsive, or imperfect to be a disciple. We are not doubting ourselves, folks, we're doubting Jesus, who said, "Trust me. Trust God" (John 14:1).

Back to the scene on the hillside.

Toward evening, the disciples encouraged Jesus to send the crowds away to surrounding villages to get food. According to John 6:6, Jesus already knew what His plan was for feeding the crowd.

The 13th Disciple

Somewhere among the thousands of people, Andrew, the brother of Peter, had discovered a boy whose mother had had the foresight to pack some food for him. We don't hear any more about the boy after the disciples have the food, but what an act of kindness for him to give it up. He had just enough food to satisfy his own appetite, but when he handed it over to Jesus, it was multiplied many times over. Maybe he had more faith in what the Teacher could do than the disciples had? Their assessment of the situation was this: "Hey, Jesus, this boy has four small barley loaves of bread and two fish, but that won't go far."

Jesus took control of the seating arrangements. If I'd be transported back in time as the 13th disciple, that would be my task. Managing hungry crowds for twenty-five years, I grew quite adept at getting as many people as possible seated in the available space. My food cost was appreciably higher, however, than Jesus'.

What happened with that single picnic lunch is what can happen with your and my talents. We can hold them tightly and use them solely for our personal gain, or we can take that leap of faith and give whatever we have to offer to Jesus. If Jesus can turn water into wine and one meal into thousands of meals, He can certainly turn our watered-down talents into a fine vintage that touches many lives.

· · ·

A string of tour buses lined the side of the highway, sending billows of smoke and fumes into the environment. (Yes, we've jumped back to the current century.)

The Church of the Multiplication of Loaves and Fishes has been built in Tabgha. The modern church was built over the remains of at least two earlier churches. This was the pattern I found throughout my hike. Wherever a location was determined to be the "probable" site of an event associated with Jesus, a church was built. Often, there was more than one church. Several denominations might have chapels or churches in the area.

Tourists of all nationalities milled about. I think it's safe to assume they also represented many religions.

As we meandered among the groups of tourists, I noticed an animated conversation between two bus drivers. One was a Jewish driver, the other a Muslim driver. As we passed, the Jewish driver took note of our backpacks.

"Where are you from?" he asked.

"America," we told him.

The United States' 2016 presidential election was coming up in a few days. We had numerous conversations with folks, especially soldiers, about our election. Many folks in Israel had more interest in it than did some of our U.S. citizens. Israel does have good reason to be concerned. Our foreign policies have repercussions for Israel's national security.

The Jewish driver was a secular Jew. Not all Jews adhere to the dictates of the Torah. In Israel, as in America, there are conservative and liberal Jews.

We told the Jewish driver that we supported the candidate we felt was more sympathetic to Israel.

He informed *us* that one candidate was bad, and the other one, worse. "All politics is corrupt," he said. "Here in Israel, as well."

Our reply was that we believed God had everything under control, and the right candidate would get elected.

He scorned that belief. "God? There is no God."

This man studied neither the Bible, Torah, nor any other religious book. He had no use for religion.

The Muslim driver jumped in with his opinion. He didn't like either candidate. He didn't like any politician in Israel, Palestine, or any other country.

"I don't like any of them. I don't even like myself," he said, as he stomped up the bus steps. Judging from the stern look on his face, I do believe he didn't like himself or anyone else on the bus, in the country, and possibly on the face of the earth.

With that bit of negativity, we took our leave. *Way too many people here.* The disciples probably said the same thing as they beached the boat and looked in dismay across the waiting crowd.

Mark tells us, though, that Jesus had a different reaction: He was moved with compassion for these people who so desperately needed Him.

CHAPTER 13

Capernaum

As we neared Capernaum, a short flight of metal steps led upward to a site on the side of a hill. This area on the Mount of Beatitudes is the traditional site of the Sermon on the Mount.

A church has been built here, too. Octagonal, its eight sides represent the eight beatitudes. A dome rises above the altar, and just below the dome are eight stained glass windows, each proclaiming one of the blessings in Latin.

The hillside overlooks the Sea of Galilee, the plain and the beach below, and Capernaum. As I wandered about the hillside, I discovered an answer to something that often puzzled me: On those days when thousands of people had congregated, how did everyone hear as Jesus spoke? They certainly didn't have the use of our modern sound systems.

We read in the Gospels that Jesus sometimes took a boat offshore and spoke to the crowd from there. Sound travels well over water. As I was standing on the hillside, quite a distance from the shore, I clearly heard a conversation between two people down on the beach. The sound naturally funneled up through the grassy amphitheater.

I tried to imagine myself in the scene: the 13th disciple, on the periphery of the action, not quite knowing how or where he should fit into what was happening that day as the people kept arriving and asking where they could find the Teacher. It occurred to me that maybe the Twelve weren't all huddled close around Jesus, listening raptly to everything He had to say—as I had always imagined the scene. It's possible they were spread out over the hillside, helping folks to find a place to sit, talking with them, directing them to the area for children's church ... No, that's my modern mind interjecting itself too much into this account.

. . .

I was lingering on the fringes of it all, wondering what I could do to be a good disciple and help out, when Jesus began speaking.

I was at a good spot, halfway up the slope, and I could hear Jesus plainly and see the reactions throughout the crowd. Some were listening with beaming faces, almost as though a holy light was shining into their souls. They were not distracted by the children occasionally jumping up or rolling around in the grass. They did not notice other people walking through, trying to find a spot to sit. They were intent on Jesus' words, soaking up everything He said.

But Jesus was not ten minutes into His teaching before I also saw some brows furrowed, some mouths pinched tight, and a few heads shaking. Several people were whispering to each other.

I admit, I felt some confusion, too. These were people whose history had seen one country after another conquer them, persecute them, and oppose their religion. Most of these folks were in attendance because they had heard that this man could possibly be the man God had finally sent to deliver their nation from a pagan ruler and establish a new kingdom. This man had the power to heal and deal with demons. Was He also there to break oppression and give them freedom? Something exciting was happening, and they were curious and hopeful.

Jesus words were radical and revolutionary, but they were not what people expected to hear. They're not what I expected to hear.

He opened with eight points on happiness. His blueprint for happiness was quite different—almost the opposite—of what folks were accustomed to hearing and thinking.

He was talking about things like poverty, mourning, meekness, hunger and thirst, mercy, and purity. He was not pushing revolution and social reform and new governments. He was, instead, focusing on each individual's inner condition.

I forgot about watching the crowd as what Jesus was saying started to hit my own heart. The meek will inherit the earth? The reward sounded good to me, but what, exactly, does it mean to be *meek?*

I whipped out my smart phone and looked it up.

One of Webster's definitions for *meek* is *spineless.*

I did not like the sound of that.

But I did like the promise of the rewards for living according to Jesus' blueprint: gaining the Kingdom of Heaven, comfort from God, inheriting the earth, justice, mercy, seeing God, being called the children of God ...

Wait.

What had He just said?

Be happy and very glad when people mock you and persecute you and lie about you and say all sorts of evil things about you because you are following Me.

This perplexed me and made me more than a little uneasy. I looked around (isn't that what we often do when we feel conviction prodding us? It's so much easier to look at others instead of our own hearts and lives). I looked around and saw that other people in the crowd were also perplexed and uncomfortable.

It's not easy to accept this teaching. No one wants lies told about them or insults thrown at them. I'm sure many of you have had this happen, whether in the workplace, home, or church. Our natural impulse—that impure heart, if you will—immediately wants to fight back. But Jesus is telling us to be glad about lies and insults. God will bless us, there will be a reward for us, and the persecution puts us in good company, with all the other folks aligned with God and maligned by the world. It puts us in Jesus' camp. Nobody was lied about more and insulted more than Jesus. Just as the devil came after the man Jesus, he'll come after us, too.

Then I realized that Jesus had just given the main point of His sermon: His disciples were to be salt and light to the world. And we're to live this way to bring praise to our Heavenly Father. Yes, that inspired me. That is what I wanted to be and do.

But then Jesus dived into the hard things again. He was talking about the practical parts of living: anger, conflict, forgiveness, lust, divorce, swearing, and revenge. All those things that can trip us up on a daily basis.

I saw even more doubt creep into the crowd when Jesus said that if an evil person slaps you, then turn the other cheek and give him another opportunity. This was not what people wanted to hear. But Jesus spoke with authority. There was no room for waffling in His teachings. He went on to talk about loving the enemy. *Do good and pray for the enemy.*

Uh-oh.

"In this way, you will be acting as true children of your Father in Heaven," Jesus said, and His words rang out over the entire hillside.

There was more. About having faith in the Heavenly Father to provide all we need. About not striving to pile up treasures here on earth but working for treasures in Heaven. About praying, giving to the needy, and not judging others.

I felt overwhelmed. This was what Jesus expects of us? He *was* asking people to sign up for a total change of lifestyle. I didn't understand it all. I knew I could not possibly live up to that standard. It was too radical. I didn't even *want* to hear all of that. It was hard enough to try to follow all the rules of my conservative church, but Jesus said my righteousness had to be even better than that of the teachers of religious law. How was that possible?

I saw some people leaving, talking among themselves.

I was deflated. I no longer felt qualified to be the 13th disciple.

. . .

Jesus often told parables—short stories with lessons that applied to people's lives. Folks didn't always understand what a parable meant. Even the disciples were mystified at times and had to ask Jesus to explain further.

This day, the parable was about a farmer going out to sow seed. Jesus spoke about birds eating up the seeds that were scattered along the path. Some seed fell into good, productive soil, but Jesus also had some thorns and rocky soil in the story, too.

You'd think His listeners would easily relate to these allegories, since there was agriculture, thorns, and certainly rocky soil in the area. But most apparently didn't grasp what this teaching was about.

Of course, the 13th disciple has heard this parable explained dozens, if not hundreds, of times. But even the twelve disciples needed an explanation. I believe Jesus got a bit frustrated with His group of fishermen and tax collectors.

"You really don't understand this parable? If you don't understand one that is so apparent, how will you ever understand any of them?" He asked them.

As Craig and I traversed the pathway from Nazareth to Capernaum, we witnessed all of those conditions. We passed through areas thick with thorns. In contrast, some soil grew bananas, tomatoes, and olive trees in abundance.

As we walked through yet one more area where trash littered and bordered the pathway, I wondered if Jesus could have taught a parable on trash. I'm sure I could. Craig gave it some thought, then spoke his own parable about God not seeing us as trash.

My friend is a successful preacher of the Gospel, but his parable didn't quite reach the Jesus level. On second thought, maybe it did—the 13th disciple didn't grasp the trash parable any better than the other twelve had understood the sower parable.

. . .

After leaving the Mount of Beatitudes, we had a short road walk to Capernaum. This was the location of Jesus Ministries, LLC. Or, perhaps, where the Jesus Corporation was first established.

It seems the Jesus business is big business today. In a parking area, buses disgorged humanity from all tribes, arriving from almost every nation.

Even during Jesus' time, business was thriving in Capernaum. With a population of about fifteen hundred, the town's location made it a crossroads of commerce. In addition, when you think about all the folks from the Decapolis, Jerusalem, and other surrounding areas who arrived there for the healing crusade, you can imagine that Capernaum and nearby villages took advantage of the business brought by all those travelers.

Jesus was walking along one day and passed a toll booth. At the table sat Levi, collecting the tolls. Now, Levi was a Jew, but he was working for the hated Roman government. That tells you something about the man, doesn't it?

His name implies that he might have been from the Levite tribe. The Levites were priestly people, a line that God had charged with being the spiritual leaders of Israel. We don't know that this toll collector was actually a Levite; but even if he was not, can you imagine his family's shame that he was working for the Romans?

Not only that, but he was probably a crooked businessman, extorting excessive fees from his fellow countrymen. Levi owed a certain amount to the government, but whatever additional money he could get was his. He could charge any road tax he wanted, and it was a lucrative business, since a major trade route passed through Capernaum. Needless to say, these tax collectors were hated by fellow Jews. In most Jewish minds, Levi and his friends in the tax-collecting business were all lumped into one category: "sinners"!

Jesus knew Levi's story. And for some reason, Jesus invited him to be a disciple.

I've often wondered how Levi—also known to us as Matthew—could leave such a lucrative post. Could it be that he was tired of being an outcast, reviled by his fellow Jews? Or was his conscience bothering him a bit, and when Jesus gave him a chance to change his life, he grabbed at the hope? Whatever his story, Jesus knew this man *needed* to be a disciple.

As a matter of fact, Matthew then invited Jesus and his other disciples to dinner and a party with Matthew's friends and business associates. When the Jewish religious leaders saw this, they criticized Jesus for associating with "such scum" (Matthew 9:11 in the New Living Translation).

Jesus spoke up.

"This is why I've come. For the sick. For those who know they need me. I'm not interested in calling those who think they are perfect."

Jesus had come to the world to help the likes of Matthew! I'm sure Matthew's ears heard that, because he knew he was scum.

I hear it, too.

. . .

One thing had not changed from ancient Capernaum to modern times. As we entered Capernaum, we were also stopped at a toll booth. Ten shekels to enter.

We were seeking admission to the area known as historic Capernaum.

In 1894, the Franciscan Friars purchased two-thirds of the area encompassing ancient Capernaum. The Greek Orthodox Church purchased the other third. Excavation was begun on the area, and one important discovery was a synagogue. Close to the synagogue and the lake shore, the Franciscan excavators found what remained of small housing units; one of those buildings was believed to be the home of Simon Peter and his mother-in-law. (One would assume his wife dwelt there as well.)

Archaeology attempted to trace the history of Peter's house. It appears that updates were made to the dwelling soon after Jesus' death, making additions that were not normally found in homes at the time. This led to the speculation that the building might have been used as a meeting place for an early church. More renovations were made in the fourth century. In the fifth century, an octagonal church was built over the site.

Should Pete get a chance to return to his ancient home today, he might have trouble locating it. He would first need to navigate the church erected there centuries ago. Then, glancing upward, he would be shocked to discover yet another structure perched overhead.

In 1990, the Franciscans built an edifice held aloft by concrete pillars. It looks like a spacecraft hovering over the remains of the old Peter homestead. If you've been on one of the glass-bottomed boats in Silver Springs State Park in Florida, you can imagine this church. Folks can peer down through the glass floor to the layers of the past. Peter, standing in his old bedroom and looking up, would likely see many faces from nations he had never heard of. Why it is permissible for a structure to be built over such a historic site bewilders me. However, as the slogan declares, ownership has its privileges.

· · ·

Black basalt rock was plentiful in the Capernaum area, and millstones and grinding stones were produced there, made out of the rock that looks something like coal. We saw millstones in many sizes on display.

I imagined the day that Jesus was walking through town and saw such a display of millstones. They were very heavy; some of the larger sizes could only be moved by two or more people.

Jesus had just warned that, while His followers will always face temptation to sin, the one who presents the temptation will suffer great punishment. He pointed toward the millstones.

"If you cause anyone who trusts Me to sin, you'd be better off having that millstone tied around your neck and be thrown out to sea."

I stood there with the ruins of Capernaum before me and the Sea of Galilee several hundred feet behind me, and I could feel the severity of Jesus' warning.

. . .

In 1925, the Franciscans reconstructed a synagogue that had been built sometime between the second and fourth centuries. Whether the location of the new building was the precise location of the synagogue where Jesus first taught is debatable. But no one can debate the impact of Jesus' first appearance there.

Mark tells the story in the very first chapter of his book. Jesus had just picked his disciples and returned to Capernaum. On the Sabbath, He went to the synagogue to teach. Folks were astonished because they noted that He taught with great authority. Something about this man and His teaching was very different from what they were accustomed to hearing.

One man in attendance was possessed by an evil spirit. Can you imagine that? Satan has his demons doing undercover work in the synagogue.

But as Jesus taught, the evil spirit, in great agitation, cried out, "Why are you interfering with us? I know who you are—you are Jesus of Nazareth, the Holy One of God!"

Jesus silenced him and ordered him out of the man. The spirit screamed and threw the man on the ground in a convulsion, but obeyed Jesus' command to leave.

The people were amazed. Mark wrote that they were wondering

what kind of new teaching this might be. Isn't it amazing that the people were so accustomed to laws, rules, and regulations that they couldn't quite grasp who Jesus really was, but the spirit of the world certainly knew!

I have to ask: Are we locked into thinking that keeps us from knowing Jesus?

After leaving the synagogue, Jesus went next door (or just down the street) to Peter's house, where Peter's mother-in-law was in bed with a fever. Jesus dismissed the fever, and the lady got to work, waiting on Jesus and the disciples.

That day seemed to light a wildfire along the grapevine, spreading the news that there was a man who was teaching new things and could heal sickness and purge folks of demons. Even before sundown on the same day, folks were appearing on Peter's doorstep, coming to either be healed or watch the healings. The second chapter of Mark relates one event where the house was so crowded that Jesus and His disciples couldn't even eat. Regardless of what they might have believed about *who* Jesus was, suffering folks who heard the rumors about His power to heal were quick to seek Him out. Their diseases and demons were enough reason for them to come.

The Teacher from Nazareth was creating quite a stir in Capernaum. Word soon reached Jerusalem. Jesus was teaching things beyond the normal law and traditions. Scribes from Jerusalem heard about what was going on in Galilee and pronounced Jesus possessed by the devil.

His family, too, heard about what Jesus was doing and teaching and showed up one day "to take custody of him," claiming Jesus was out of His mind. How was it possible that the people who were probably the closest to Him for thirty years still didn't realize He was the Son of God? Or maybe they did know, but were embarrassed

123

by the way Jesus was so blatantly stepping outside their traditions? What was Mary thinking? I don't think she could have forgotten the visit from the angel and the promise Gabriel had given her, or the prophecies from Anna and Simeon in the Temple.

We also wonder how the disciples could have seen the lame walk, the blind being given sight, and even the dead brought back to life and still have doubts about who Jesus was. But as I sought to better understand what it means to follow Jesus, I read the Gospels again and journaled my thoughts, and I admit that doubt began to creep into my own mind. Was what I had been taught all these years accurate? Was Jesus possibly a bit deranged? Did He just have a God complex of some sort?

Demons finally made me realize that Jesus was who He said He was.

Yes, demons.

Whenever Jesus cast out demons and evil spirits, they immediately knew who they were facing. Time and again they would call out, "You are the Son of God!" The spirit world knew exactly who Jesus was and what authority He held.

As I hiked Israel and walked where Jesus had walked, the humanity of Jesus became real. He felt hunger, pain, joy, grief, and yes, even temptation. Every emotion I have felt, Jesus felt. Every temptation I've met, Jesus met as well. His track record is perfect, though, while mine is a bit flawed.

Who is Jesus to you? Just another well-schooled man? A great prophet? Even Muslim folks believe Jesus does have a place in history as a great prophet. (They believe their prophet is greater, though.)

Everyone must decide for themselves who they believe Jesus was. Was He a crazy individual who captured the nation's attention for a while? Or was He the Son of God in human flesh and blood? Those are your two choices. Your eternal destiny rests on your decision. The choice is *that* important.

. . .

In a small gift shop in Capernaum, cases of pomegranate fruit were piled high. Two men were working at hand-operated juicers, pressing pomegranate juice to sell to passersby. For five American dollars (which sounded like less than the stated price of eighteen shekels), one could have a large glass of pomegranate juice.

The pomegranate has always been a special fruit in Israel. Some people believe that this was the fruit Eve picked in the Garden of Eden. Jewish tradition states that there are 613 seeds in one fruit, and each seed corresponds to one of the 613 commandments that Orthodox Jews are to follow. I didn't count the seeds myself, but I did read elsewhere that pomegranates have over 800 seeds. Perhaps that 800 also includes the rules I was commanded to follow. (That might be stretching the facts, though. The list of rules I was given probably numbered the same as the seeds in an apple.)

You'll find many references to pomegranates in the Scriptures. The speaker in Song of Solomon 6:11 mentions going to see if the pomegranates were in bloom. In 1 Kings 7, we read details of the design of Solomon's temple, including pomegranates engraved on the pillars. Going back even further in Israel's history, when the Lord gave Moses detailed instructions about priestly robes, He instructed that the hem of the priest's garments were to be adorned with pomegranates, woven in blue, purple, and scarlet yarn. To my mind, the fact that God specified that pomegranates be used in the Temple design and the priest's robes makes this fruit a special symbol. Today, the pomegranate is still considered to represent knowledge and wisdom, so it's often eaten on the Jewish New Year.

So I slapped down five dollars and had my first taste of real pomegranate juice. Depending on the size of the fruit, three, four, or five whole pomegranates are cut in half and then the life is squeezed out of all those little seeds. The press is a hand-operated contraption with a handle that looks much like an old pump handle.

After my trip to Israel, I purchased a fruit press in order to squeeze my own fresh knowledge-and-wisdom juice every morning at home in the States. Once I had the press, and in great anticipation of the enhanced mental and physical health I was about to achieve, I approached the produce buyer at our local supermarket and informed him I wished to order a case of pomegranates.

"Out of season," he said. "We only have those in the fall, probably around October."

I have discovered the press does juice oranges quite well.

CHAPTER 14

The Far Country

We were headed for the far country.

Leaving Capernaum, our next destination was a kibbutz named Ein Gev, a settlement located in the Decapolis area, approximately where Jesus came ashore following the storm He had first slept through and then quieted.

We were no longer on the Jesus Trail. That trail ended in Capernaum. Another blazed trail did circle the Sea of Galilee, and we determined that following this new trail would get us to Ein Gev in time to have St. Peter's fish for supper.

I had read about this famous fish served in area restaurants. One seafood restaurant located near the kibbutz seemed a likely place to sample the dish.

A tax collector in Capernaum cornered Peter one day and asked if Jesus had paid His temple tax. Peter took the question to Jesus, who replied that He was tax-exempt, but—just so that no one would be offended—He would pay. It's a strange story; okay, call it a fish story if you want. Because Jesus then sent Peter fishing. Not to catch fish to sell and make a little money to pay the taxes. No, that wasn't the reason Peter was to go fish.

"Toss out a line, Peter. Reel that fish in. Pry open its mouth and there will be enough cash to pay taxes for us both." Those were Jesus' instructions.

It seems a strange miracle, compared to healing, casting out demons, and quieting violent storms. Why did Jesus choose to supply their need in such an unusual way? He certainly proved His power, but *a coin in the mouth of a fish?* I'll have to ask Jesus for further elaboration on that one, too.

That story is what caused St. Peter's Fish to appear on the menu of many local eateries.

The fish that has supplied sustenance for people in Israel for several thousand years is tilapia. It's probably the fish that Jesus used to feed the five thousand.

. . .

The Sea of Galilee is the largest freshwater lake in Israel. As we began our circumnavigation of the lake, we could see evidence that the water level had dropped drastically over the years. Some folks blame that on global warming or climate change, but there are other more obvious explanations.

The lake supplies nearly a third of the drinking water for the entire country. Agriculture also draws large amounts of water from the lake for irrigation. We saw the results of this: Lush flowers bloomed profusely along roadsides; citrus and banana groves stretched out across the landscape. We hiked through these groves for miles and miles.

Israel is part of a pact between neighboring countries who each have a share in the water of the Jordan River, which begins in the Golan Heights. Back in 1965, the Syrian government came up with a plan to divert much of the water flowing out of the Golan Heights, preventing the water from reaching the Sea of Galilee. That would have been catastrophic for Israel. Access to water was also at stake in the 1967 war, which began with fighting between Egypt and Israel but escalated when Syria entered the fray. When Israel captured the Golan Heights, they were protecting their water source.

The Sea of Galilee is about 140 feet deep at its maximum depth. It is also the lowest freshwater lake in the world, and the second-lowest lake in the world, second only to the Dead Sea, where the water exiting the Sea of Galilee eventually ends up.

Beneath the Sea of Galilee, salt springs bubble up. The heavier fresh water keeps that salt water confined. However, there is a danger that if too much fresh water is siphoned off the lake, it's possible that the salt springs would then make the water undrinkable. Israel is at the forefront of research, development, and construction of desalination plants to turn the salt water of the Mediterranean Sea into drinking water.

We were headed to the source of it all, the point where the Jordan River originates from springs and snow melt at the base of Mt. Hermon in the Golan Heights.

· · ·

In Proverbs 30, verses 24 to 26, the writer speaks of four things on earth that are small but wise. One of the creatures mentioned is the cony. Psalm 104:18 informs us that conies live in crags, or rock formations.

Conies is the King James word. Other translations use *hyraxes, rock badgers,* or *shephanim.* None of those names meant anything to me.

But as we walked along the seaside, we passed an area dotted with rock formations, and peering at us warily or darting through the rocks and brush were these creatures. Conies are similar in size and color to a woodchuck. Their heads look something like a fox, and so they're a bit more attractive than a groundhog. Conies do not burrow, though. They live among the rocks, seemingly a wise choice for an animal the Proverbs writer calls a "feeble folk."

To me they looked like a "lazy folk," lying around and catching rays. They are very skittish, though, and sentries will whistle or chatter to warn of approaching danger. Perhaps the sentries are also part of the wisdom that Proverbs was admiring.

The colony scampering among and lying on the rocks was quite large. After sensing that we posed no danger, the critters just sat there and observed us as we observed them. I approached several and got quite close before they retreated to the safety of their craggy fortress.

. . .

The sound of flowing water could be heard, although we could not see the source. The Jordan River was somewhere off to our right. We approached a road crossing, and a short distance ahead, a sign made a simple announcement: *Jordan.*

On Jordan's stormy banks I stood and cast a wishful eye. The old song says my eye goes *to Canaan's fair and happy land where my possessions lie.* But that night, my possessions were going to lie across the river, opposite from Canaan's land.

When the second generation of Israelites who had fled Egypt

stood at the Jordan River and looked at the land of Canaan, they were casting their wishful eyes on land already occupied by clans who were descendants of Canaan, the son of Ham and grandson of Noah. Genesis 10 lists those tribes for us: the Sidonians, Hittites, Jebusites, Amorites, Girgashites, Hivites, Arkites, Sinites, Arvadites, Zemarites, and Hamathites.

You will remember that Noah had three sons: Shem, Ham, and Japheth. Canaan was the son of Ham. The Israelites who were arriving to claim their promised land were descendants of Israel, son of Abraham, a descendant of Shem.

Joshua, Moses' successor in leadership, was commanded to cross over the Jordan and with help from God drive all other tribes out of Canaan. It was as though, after many generations, the will had been opened and God said that one line of descendants of Shem were now to inherit the land that Ham's family had been living on for generations.

The promised inheritance included Syria, Lebanon, and Jordan. Not everyone will agree with me, but I believe this settles the argument as to what land belongs to the nation of Israel.

In the discussion about who has the rights to what land and who was "there first," some choose to go back only a few centuries to establish ownership; they set down a marker at a certain point in history and believe the Palestinian people have the right to the land.

I'll give some grace to people who don't believe the Bible, but anyone who claims to believe that the Scriptures are God's Word and that God is sovereign should not have any doubts as to who is the rightful landowner. Prophecies contain severe warnings for countries who wish to deprive Israel of their inheritance. During the 1967 war when Israel was attacked, God did seem to intervene and give Israel a great victory. They conquered much of the territory, but in subsequent peace treaties gave much of it back. They still hold the Golan Heights, a strategic position.

Let's also remind ourselves that the word *Palestine* has changed in its meaning. Originally, it referred only to the seacoast area of the land of Canaan, where the Philistines lived. Gradually, the name was used to include larger areas until, by a time that most of my generation can remember, it meant the entire territory we also called *the Holy Land or the land of Israel.* Not until the 1960s did the term *Palestinians* begin to be used for the population (not a country) of non-Jews, usually Arabic-speaking and Muslim, who oppose the nation of Israel. Yes, it's complicated.

. . .

As the Israelites stepped forward to cross the Jordan River, the waters stopped flowing and backed up, overflowing the riverbanks for a long distance.

That river crossing took place south of the Sea of Galilee. I was standing on the banks of the mighty Jordan north of the Sea of Galilee, and I cast my own wishful eye and contemplated the two options of crossing. The obvious option was the bridge near where we stood. The second option was to go down beside the bridge, get a running start, and leap over the river. In my younger years, I believe I could have made the jump. I probably would have splashed down a bit short of the other bank though. But that at least gives you an idea of what the Jordan looks like nearer its source.

The Jordan River is not what it used to be. There would be no need to stop the waters for us. Too many people have drawn off its waters upstream to cause any stormy banks where we stood.

However, we did use the bridge.

We must have cast our wishful eyes too much on the distant land, since we lost sight of the blazes marking the trail around the lake. With no idea where the trail should be, we opted for a road walk and decided to try hitchhiking.

Before we even had a chance to raise our hands for a ride, we noticed a pickup truck parked off the roadway to our right. It was the time for prayer. Two men wandered about while the third man was kneeling on the shoulder of the road, praying in the direction of Mecca.

At the conclusion of the prayer meeting, we inquired if we could jump on the back of the pickup and have a ride to Kibbutz Ein Gev.

The praying man seemed to be in charge of decision making. The two non-praying men asked the prayer warrior whether he would take us to our destination.

He shook his head *no*.

We offered to pay him.

The answer was still an emphatic negative.

These Muslim fellows apparently didn't subscribe to the Jewish command of *mitzvah*, doing good deeds.

We continued walking down the highway for several miles with our arms outstretched and our hopes high that someone would give us a ride. It was a busy highway, and cars and trucks whizzed by without stopping.

At an area off to the side of the highway, Craig spotted a brushy area that he felt would conceal him from traffic while he answered the call of nature. He disappeared.

An exclamation came from the bushes.

"You need to see the sign posted here!"

The spot he had chosen as a safe comfort station was posted with a yellow sign. Capital letters warned, DANGER, MINES!

No thanks, I can wait!

For a few more miles we plodded along the busy shoulder of the highway. Hitchhiking proved futile. We reached an intersection where we found another road leading toward Ein Gev. As we approached, I spotted a small café across the road, set back from the traffic. I suggested we go there, take a break, and possibly get information about a ride.

Reaching the café entrance, we realized that the building was vacant. Out of business.

Things didn't seem to be working out too well.

Just then, a car pulled into the parking lot. Three young men also peered into the café in hopes of finding refreshment.

"I think that's the ride God sent for us. It's worth a try," I said.

Craig and I approached the car and asked if they could give us a ride to Ein Gev. We did not hold high hopes; we had noted that they had just come from that direction, and why would they be willing to turn around and go back toward Ein Gev again?

Their English was good enough that we could communicate quite well.

"We will pay you to drive us to Ein Gev."

They replied, "No, no," and shook their heads.

Disappointed and rejected by both Muslims and Jews in the space of several hours, we turned around to leave.

Then one of the men shouted at us.

"Get in!" he said, holding the door open and motioning us toward the car.

We had misunderstood. The head shaking and the negative reply was in response to the suggestion of payment. We had actually insulted them by offering money. They would take us, as a *mitzvah*. They were doing a good deed, on a mission from God. These young men had been trained by their parents to do good deeds with no thought of gaining something in return.

As we drove, we learned that the young men were on a break from their military service and were just out driving around and enjoying their time off. Their first question to us was one we would hear almost every time we were given a ride: "Who are you for in the upcoming election in America?" The Israeli people are probably more informed about U.S. politics than most of our own citizens.

God's taxi dropped us off at the entrance to Kibbutz Ein Gev, at the base of the Golan Heights.

The meaning of *Ein Gev* is *spring of the cistern.* This kibbutz is a famous and popular holiday resort, with a hotel, restaurant, and small cottages stretched along the eastern shore of the Sea of Galilee. Its location is almost directly across the lake from the hotel in Capernaum where we had stayed the previous night.

A kibbutz is a farm where a number of families live a communal lifestyle. Israel has nearly three hundred kibbutzim, and Ein Gev is one of the wealthiest. This kibbutz includes banana plantations, dairy farms, tourist accommodations, and a famous fish restaurant. If you ever get the opportunity to visit Israel, by all means, go to the far country and visit Kibbutz Ein Gev.

The hotel rooms had already been filled by busloads of tourists, but one of the holiday houses was available for the night. It could be ours if we were willing to part with a great number of shekels. We thought we must surely be purchasing the cottage, but it turned out to be only a one-night rental. The king's ransom did include a breakfast buffet in the resort's large dining hall.

The Harbor Fish Restaurant came highly recommended and is famous for its St. Peter's Fish. That was definitely where we wanted to consume our evening meal. We were informed that walking along the highway to the restaurant would be dangerous at night, so the innkeeper scheduled a van to pick us up later in the evening.

Before supper, I wanted to get down to the seashore, go back in time, and observe the arrival of Jesus and the disciples. They were also crossing to the far country, coming to the land of pig farmers to deal with one man in dire need of help. We had heard that their boat had been caught up in a vicious storm about mid-lake.

I was on the shore as the sun slipped below the horizon. Diagonally across the lake, lights from the hillside town of Tiberius shimmered in the evening glow.

As I took in the beautiful views and listened to the waves lapping the sand, the wind picked up. At once, what had been a soothing greeting between waves and sand became an angry, hostile meeting. The stronger wind and the slapping of the waves made it easy to visualize the disciples in the boat, still far from land, leaning against the oars as the wind howled and the waves grew ever larger, eventually breaking over the boat and nearly swamping it. These men who, I assume, had been on the water most of their lives were frightened. The storm was getting uglier by the moment.

Through all of this, Jesus slept.

The shortest verse in the Bible is "Jesus wept," found in John 11:35. "Jesus slept" would have been a good challenger to the title of Shortest Verse if it had only been written that way. It still would have finished second, though, since it has one additional letter.

However, I digress from the scene at hand.

Jesus was awakened by the frightened disciples and immediately issued the command: "Quiet! Be still!"

Calmness fell over the lake as the wind and waves died down.

Are you ever at a point in life where it feels like you will be overwhelmed by the storms? I'm sure many of us have been in these frightening situations—or are, right now. Does it seem like Jesus is asleep and does not care about your well-being?

Perhaps your faith is being tested, perhaps the trial you are going through is to prepare you to become a disciple as well. We usually don't know the reason God allows the storm to batter our boats.

But if Jesus is in your boat, He is willing and able to say to the waves buffeting your faith, "Quiet! Be Still!"

Photo Section

Ancient street in Nazareth

Olive grove

Cana

Minaret in Cana

Magdala from Mt Arbel

The climb down Mt Arbel

Banana grove

Sea of Galilee

Photo Section

Mount of Beatitudes

Capernaum

Millstones

First glimpse of Jordan River

Danger sign

St. Peter's fish

Kibbutz Ein Gev

The Golan Heights

Photo Section

Golan Heights Hostel

Temple of Pan

Beginnings of Jordan River

Walls of Old Jerusalem

The 13th Disciple

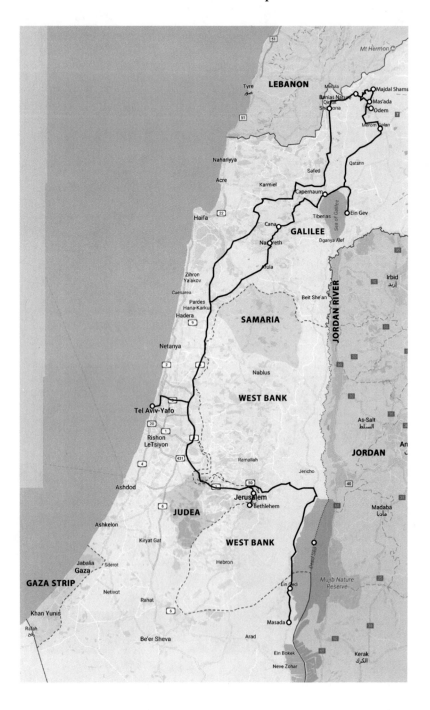

Photo Section

Golden menorah

Praying at the Western Wall

Sealed Golden Gate

Damascus Gate

The 13ᵗʰ Disciple

Garden of Gethsemane

Street in Old City

Ein Gedi

Street market

Photo Section

Garden Tomb

In the tomb

At the Wall Friday night

Arriving for prayers

CHAPTER 15

Pigs in the Far Country

As I stood by the sea, contemplating the events about to unfold, a figure moved into my peripheral vision. At the same time, a horrible, chilling sound reached my ears.

The inhuman howls came from a man roaming about the caves of a nearby burial ground. The howls alternated with screams and strings of incoherent words. As a visitor in the area, I'd been warned about this man. Folks in town had tried chaining him down to keep him under control, to no avail. He broke the chains. Day and sleepless night found him roaming about, cutting himself with sharp rocks. I'd been advised just to keep my distance if I see him.

I determined that there was still plenty of distance between us. If he headed my way, I had time to turn and run. Although, if he was supernaturally strong, I supposed I couldn't outrun him. But being from the future, I knew what was about to happen and that such a chase was not part of the actual account, so I felt safe just standing and watching. Happily, help was on the way.

For the moment, though, I was shocked by the misery and hopelessness of the man's condition.

As I watched him, something out on the lake caught his attention—several boats were gliding toward the shore. It was the boats bringing Jesus and His disciples. (Why I was not on that boat, too, as the 13th disciple, I don't know.)

The man began running, wildly and carelessly, like an animal. He was headed toward the spot on the beach where the first boat would touch the sand.

Several of the disciples had jumped out, splashing into the water, to pull the boat up on the sand. I could see Jesus, standing in the bow. He had seen the wild man and quietly watched his approach.

As Jesus stepped out onto the sand, the man darted up to Him. The disciples took a few steps back; the man did have a fearsome look. But before any words could be exchanged, Jesus addressed the spirit in the man. His voice held authority that no earthly or heavenly being could question.

"You! Evil spirit! Come out of this man!"

From within the man came another chilling, inhuman shriek.

"What do you want with me, Jesus, Son of the Most High God? Why are you here? Swear to God that you won't torture me!"

Humans were having a difficult time deciding what to believe about Jesus, but demons of the spiritual world knew exactly who He was. And they knew He was more powerful than they.

"What's your name?" Jesus asked.

"Legion. There are many of us in here."

A *legion* in the Roman army was two thousand men. Could there have been thousands of demons in that man?

The voice, on behalf of all the demons, begged again and again not to be sent out of the area. The demons even dared to suggest to

Jesus that He send them into the herd of pigs on a nearby hillside. Again, these spiritual powers recognized the authority of Jesus. They may have been working for Satan, but when Jesus arrived, He had the final word.

Jesus granted their request, and off they went, into the unsuspecting swine. There must have been at least two thousand pigs over on that hill. One for each demon? Pigs aren't usually energetic animals, but those hogs suddenly threw up their heads, began squealing and grunting, and went charging frantically down the slope. Have you ever heard two thousand pigs squealing in panic? The swineherds were panicked, too, running everywhere, helplessly flailing their arms and wondering what had happened. The pigs could not be stopped, and they thundered down the steep hill and splashed into the water. Can pigs swim? I don't know, but these apparently could not. They struggled a few minutes, then died, while still more came behind them, plunging into the sea.

The men charged with overseeing the herd stood on the hill above, stunned, staring at the dead animals floating in the waves. They looked at each other, conferred a bit, then ran off in different directions.

My eyes went back to Jesus and His disciples. They were still on the beach, at the spot where they had disembarked.

In what seemed like only minutes, people were running up, breathless, and curious. They stopped running and stared with open mouths at the pigs floating out in the water. They looked toward the boat and then approached cautiously, because the wild man from the cemetery was still there. He was no longer a wild man, though. He was talking with Jesus, and his demeanor now seemed saner than some of those incredulous people who had come to see what was going on.

Everyone was talking about what had happened—about the

demons, the pigs, the cemetery man. People were starting to look at Jesus with awe and fear. They knew this was no ordinary man. Then … they actually asked Him to leave!

Jesus turned to get back in the boat.

The freed man begged to go with Jesus. Wouldn't you? He had been given a new life. He wanted to be with the one who had the power to restore life.

But this guy was turned down, just as I was when applying for the job of 13th Disciple. I could sympathize with him.

Then I heard Jesus tell the man what He had told me and what He says to any other person applying for the position of disciple: "Go home to your family, and tell them how much the Lord has done for you and how He has had mercy on you."

The man stood and watched as the water widened between the boat and the shore. He waved several times. Finally, he turned and started jogging in the opposite direction.

I know the rest of the story. Instead of wandering about the caves of the dead, he took to going about all the towns of the Decapolis, telling his story. Folks were amazed. They knew his past. They knew how hopeless his situation once was. Now there he was, sane, healthy, telling a story about a man who had the power to give a new life.

. . .

I can't leave this scene without a few more comments and questions.

First, this is an incredible story. Jesus went to the far country— where no "good" Jew would ever set foot—to help a man in chains. Yes, the demoniac could break physical chains. But he could not rid himself of the spiritual chains. That is exactly what Jesus can do for each one of us. He can break whatever chains bind us. He has the power and the authority. As He said in one of His first public announcements, He came to set prisoners free.

As Jesus left on this mission of mercy for one man, did Satan know that all those demons he had stashed in that man were in jeopardy? Did Satan have the power to cause that storm, hoping the boat would turn around and go back? That is, of course, conjecture on my part, but it does make me pause and wonder.

Another question: What were pigs doing in the picture?

My first reaction is: Pigs stink!

For those folks who may not have grown up on a farm or within smelling distance of pigs, let me tell you: It can get really stinky. Pigs on their own, perhaps, are not necessarily that smelly, but when they're in a confined space, the aroma is real and really bad.

My father was in the animal feed business for most of his adult life. As a young boy, I would occasionally go with him as he made his rounds to Amish farms and delivered various kinds of feed. I have great memories of those times spent with my father. Years later, when Dad announced his retirement plans, I asked to again go with him one day before he retired. I took along a video recorder, to capture the memories.

We made a delivery to an Amish pig farmer. He had a large herd of hogs in confinement, and I was in close quarters with them as Dad unloaded the feed. Unknown to me, the pigs left their mark on me.

Returning home, I looked forward to relating the day's events to my wife. I took several steps inside the house and was greeted by a commanding shout.

"Out! Now!" I was not to take one more step in her direction. "Stand out there and take off all your clothes and toss them in the direction of the washing machine. Yes! All of them!"

I didn't even know that I was polluted.

While I did as ordered, I kept thinking, *I was naked, and you took me in.* I hoped she was going to follow that directive of the Lord.

There's a lesson in that incident. I repeat: Pigs stink. But it's possible that you don't even know the odor is clinging to you.

Let's go back to the history of the Israelites.

When the tribes of Israel were camped beyond the Jordan and it was time to take possession of the Promised Land, the tribe of Gad was one of several tribes that requested to remain where they were. They had large herds of sheep and cattle, and the land was suitable for grazing.

The men of these tribes promised to go along and help conquer the lands of Canaan, even willing to be on the front lines of battle, if they could have the land they were camped on and divide it among themselves.

Their promise was accepted, they marched along with all the other tribes, and the land of Canaan was conquered. Joshua gave the two and a half tribes the land they requested east of the Jordan and exhorted them to remain faithful to God.

By the time of Jesus, these people had become pig farmers. Pigs, you'll remember, were an unclean food, forbidden to the Israelites. Over many generations, God's command against pigs was first eased, then eventually ignored by the citizens of the far country.

This is a good example of what can happen today in our own society and churches. Things that once were seen as abhorrent, practices that no Christian would ever be audacious enough to claim to be approved by God, have become acceptable in some churches. Yes, there are swineherds, keeping watch over figurative pigs in our denominations. Take care, Bride of Jesus. We can be infused by the stink if we don't stay alert.

. . .

As promised, our ride arrived at the hostel to take us to the fish house. Israel is blessed with an exceptional array of delicious dishes. One of those is tilapia.

The St. Peter's fish arrived at my table with an ornery grin on its mouth. At least, it seemed to be grinning at me. The entire fish had been tossed into a deep fryer, minus the innards, of course. Maybe the grin was more of a grimace—since it could have been contemplating what it would endure as I battled through the difficult task of separating flesh from bones.

This fish was a distant relative of the fish with a four-drachma coin in its mouth. I checked. The grinning mouth was empty. Instead of delivering drachmas to me, he cost me a good many.

Our one-mile ride to the restaurant gave us an idea: Might a ride also be available for the thirty-eight-mile trip we had planned for the next day? We asked our driver about the possibility of giving us a ride and were told that one of the kibbutz employees would be available to drive us.

Our goal for the next day was Odem, a small settlement in the Golan Heights. We arranged to leave at one o'clock the following afternoon, since we wanted to hike the hillside opposite the Ein Gev kibbutz before we left.

. . .

The Golan is a disputed area on the border between Israel, Syria, and Lebanon. It's a plateau that extends from Mt. Hermon in the north to the eastern shore of the Sea of Galilee. The Golan Heights were part of Syria until the 1967 war when Israel was attacked. Then, Israel took control of the area, and since that time over forty Israeli settlements have developed in the western two-thirds of the area. The

United Nations and many European countries consider this territory to be owned by Syria although "occupied" by Israel, and they desire for Israel to be foolish enough to give it back. There are also well-intentioned American lawmakers who have similar thoughts.

Shortly after the 1967 war, Israel passed a resolution to give land back to Syria in exchange for peace between the two nations, but Israel's neighboring countries aren't necessarily interested in peace. They want the whole of Israel. Israel did give a small portion of the Golan to act as a buffer zone, patrolled by the United Nations.

That disputed landscape was where we were headed the next day.

The small beachside cottage we had rented for the night in Kibbutz Ein Gev came with Internet connections and several large-screen televisions. While Craig searched the Internet for a hostel in the Golan Heights, I got caught up on events back home in the States. An election was about to take place, and I wanted an update on the campaign. The election was two days away, and by Election Night, I hoped to be somewhere with a television to watch the results as they came in.

The talking heads from our totally unbiased news media informed me that the election was for all intents and purposes over. Their candidate of choice couldn't possibly lose. When the unbelievable actually happened and the candidate who had no chance of winning actually did, it reminded me a bit of Israel, a small country with enemies all around it and frequently attacked but always victorious against great odds.

While I watched the news, Craig discovered a small hostel in Odem that was within fifteen miles of the Banias Nature Reserve. Within that reserve is the site of ancient Caesarea Philippi. Jesus took His disciples there shortly before departing for Jerusalem, where He knew He would be executed.

CHAPTER 16

The Golan Heights

I went to the front desk early the next morning to confirm that our ride would be there at one o'clock. I also informed the gentleman that we intended to spend the forenoon climbing the hillside where the pigs had launched their collective headlong rush to the sea. He looked at me in amazement. Just that morning, he said, a herd of pigs had been rooting around outside the motel—an unusual occurrence, judging by the incredulity in his voice.

We set out, first walking through large banana fields on the lower slope of the steep hill. Then the incline increased sharply, and we were glad for the many switchbacks that eased our climb to the top.

At the crest of the hill lie the ancient ruins of a Roman city named Susita. One of the ten cities of the Decapolis, it was also known by the Greek name of Hippos. The town was destroyed by an earthquake in the eighth century, and archaeologists are currently excavating the ruins.

This was the hillside where the demoniac had possibly roamed.

Hippos might have been the first town to hear the news about the loss of the pig herd, since it would have been the closest town—*if* this was indeed the Hill of the Great Pig Stampede.

. . .

Mathias, our driver, arrived at precisely one o'clock that afternoon. He was a young man who had just completed his three-year hitch in the Israeli military. En route to Odem, we passed several military encampments where training was taking place, and Mathias told us he had taken some of his military training in this same area.

As we approached Odem, we passed a number of empty buildings and questioned whether these buildings were also used by the military for training exercises. No, they were homes and businesses that were in Syrian control before the 1967 war; now they were abandoned.

Our hostel, the Golan Heights Hostel, was located in a beautiful forested area at the foot of Mt. Odem, a dormant volcano. The town of Odem is an Israeli settlement, a small collection of homes and a winery.

The young man who checked us into the hostel was an American, originally from Colorado. He was a preacher's kid who had soured on religion as a result of watching how people had treated his father. Craig is never one to shy away from sharing the love of Jesus, and he immediately struck up a conversation with the young man, talking about the love of God and some of the difficulties that go along with pastoring a church.

Another unique delight of overseas travel is the diversity of people one meets in small hostels in faraway places. The Golan Heights Hostel was a youth hostel, and a group of about a dozen folks from around the globe were gathered there.

We were promised a vegetarian meal that evening. To my mind and palate, that translates as *we were threatened* with the promise of a vegetarian meal.

Craig and I hoped to catch a ride to the Banias Nature Reserve yet that afternoon. Our host informed us there was no transportation available to drive us there. We'd have to hitchhike or walk. If we expended that much energy, would a dinner of only vegetables resupply all the calories we would use?

Our host mentioned that he had hitchhiked to the nature reserve the previous week and had had some difficulty getting a ride back to Odem. He didn't return until after sunset. That gave me some hope: There was a possibility that if we had similar difficulties finding a ride back, we might return too late to enjoy the vegetable puree.

We struck up a conversation with a fellow from Canada. Stewart had just reconciled with his wife, following a period of separation. Then he decided to take a six-month leave from work to go see the world. Yes, by himself! It didn't make sense to me, either.

When Stewart learned of our plans, he asked if we would mind if he joined us on the journey to Banias Nature Reserve. We didn't mind, but we did wonder about the chances of *three* men being given a ride.

First, we would have a one-mile walk to reach the main road where we hoped to find a ride.

As soon as we started walking away from the hostel, a dilemma arose. This hostel had an assortment of hound dogs wandering the grounds. Whether they belonged there or were simply village mutts roaming about, we did not know. They seemed friendly enough. One dog with some German shepherd characteristics took an instant liking to us and decided he, too, was going to join our group.

The 13ᵗʰ Disciple

The four of us took off down the road. We tried to encourage our canine friend to return to the hostel, or to at least keep his distance from us. No one in their right mind would stop to pick up three hitchhikers and a dog.

Along the road, the fields were rocky and barren. A large flock of goats searched for the sparse vegetation among these rocks, and a shepherd wandered alongside the road, keeping them from drifting onto the blacktop. One would think our hound would have better enjoyed the company of the goats rather than us humans who did not welcome him, but he was not distracted from his dedication to us.

We reached the main highway and extended our arms, inviting anyone to pick us up. We tried to chase the dog away, attempting to make it clear that he was not one of our party. Our efforts were futile. No one stopped.

This was not a great surprise.

After thirty minutes of this futility, we were about to give up. Then, finally, a white, rusty, beaten up, old Datsun pickup slowed down as it approached.

We motioned frantically, trying to communicate that the dog was not with us. *No, no dog. Just three of us need a ride.*

The driver had long dreadlocks and was the spitting image of the late reggae singer Bob Marley. Had we not been aware that Mr. Marley had passed on many years before, we would have been convinced he was living in the Golan Heights in Israel. (Would we perhaps also come face-to-face with Elvis?)

Our pseudo Bob Marley kept pointing at the dog.

We kept declaring, *No, no, just us three.*

With hand signals that we could not misinterpret, he showed us precisely why he had stopped.

He wanted the dog.

He gave an inviting shout to the beast, and the dog jumped into the cab and off they went, leaving us three humans stranded by the roadside.

We finally admitted the futility of three hikers getting a ride, and we decided to draw the curtain on that endeavor. At least, we could now be assured of returning to the hostel in time to get our ration of vegetables.

. . .

The hostel is situated at the base of Mt. Odem, the second-highest mountain in Israel. We decided that a better course of action so late in the afternoon might be to expend some calories climbing to the top of the mountain. The summit is at an elevation of just over one thousand feet, so we had no need of guides or any other assistance in our climb.

The views over the surrounding area were breathtaking. In the distance lay Mt. Hermon, where snowmelt flows down to form the waterfalls in the Banias Reserve. The most impressive of those is a thirty-three-foot waterfall that plunges into a pool studded with rocks and surrounded by lush forest.

We were also near the borders of Lebanon and Syria. Several ladies who were out walking conversed with us in broken English and sign language, pointing out borders and boundaries and telling us of the difficulties and joys of living in such a troubled area of the world.

Trees dotted the landscape below us, but the ground we stood on was a rich chocolate brown, devoid of all vegetation. There was, however, one lonely flower of pale pink and purple hues that had pushed itself up through the rocky ground. One lonely survivor in a hostile environment. I took a picture of it. It seemed to me to be a symbol of Israel.

. . .

We descended Mt. Odem as the sun slipped toward the horizon, streaking the clouds with reds and golds. The time was rapidly approaching for our vegetable meal.

Let me say first that I don't see myself becoming a vegetarian anytime soon. But I must admit, the meal that night was quite good. A variety of vegetables had been disguised as food and were actually palatable.

I was seated beside a young lady from Australia. Our conversation naturally included vegetables, and I mentioned that I'd often heard of *Vegemite,* a product that is popular in the land down under. I knew nothing more than what I've read about Vegemite or heard mentioned in song.

She immediately left the table. Soon she returned with a tube—yes, a tube—of Vegemite. It looked like a tube of toothpaste, only shorter and fatter.

"It's delicious," she remarked. "Australians love it. We make sandwiches out of it. Normally one puts it on toast, but any type of bread will work."

I tentatively put a drop of it on my finger. It had the consistency and look of a thick, dark, chocolate paste. I gave it a try.

My lips puckered. My eyes bulged. My tongue protested the vile taste.

I have sifted through my vocabulary, trying to find words to describe the taste of Vegemite. I also searched Google to see if anyone could give a better description. Here's my description first, followed by Google's attempt.

If a person took fifty gallons of soy sauce and cooked it down until nothing remained but paste, the remaining mire might be getting close to Vegemite.

A Google search for *What does Vegemite taste like?* yields this answer—and this is a word-for-word quote:

> The first option is "soy sauce," an apt description of the salty brown sludge so popular in Australia. The second is "beer," which also makes sense considering Vegemite is made from leftover brewers' yeast extract.

Yet another description from Google is that Vegemite "tastes like sadness."

The tube of "sludge" reminded me of a small container of grease my father used to grease equipment. I think, though, that my father's grease would have tasted better.

Vegemite is a byproduct of beer manufacturing. The yeast that remains after the fermentation process has taken place is mixed with salt and other spices and some secret vegetable mixture. The spread has nutritional value, according to vegetarians. It contains nutrients one would normally receive from meat.

If all this hasn't discouraged you from purchasing a tube of sadness, then by all means rush out and buy it. Get the smallest container possible, since it will last you a lifetime. It will also be an item you will be able to pass along from generation to generation. That assumes, of course, that your family doesn't reside in Australia.

Why the discourse about something as unimportant as Vegemite? Possibly because it illustrates the essence of travel: meeting new people, seeing new places, sharing strange and unusual experiences. And finding that the tasting of something quite foul was yet enjoyable when in the company of fellow sojourners.

CHAPTER 17

The Gates of Hell

I would imagine if you look back over the landscape that is your life, there will be a day or two you consider a "Big Day." Your wedding. The birth of a child. Or perhaps a day of travel when you witnessed unimagined wonders of God's creation.

The day following my vegetarian meal and Vegemite experiment was one of those days for me. Should I be blessed with rocking-chair age and a good memory, thoughts of that day will forever bring smiles.

It was a Big Day. A day of living large. It was also Election Day back in the good old U.S.A.

I wanted to be in Jerusalem by the day's end to watch the election unfold. I did not anticipate what a day we would have getting there.

Fortunately, Stewart decided to take a different hike that morning, so only Craig and I would again be attempting to hitchhike to the Banias Nature Reserve in the Caesarea Philippi area.

We left the hostel as soon as daylight appeared, wondering if anyone would pick up two strangers. We expected to walk the mile out to the main highway before we had any opportunity of getting a ride, but we were wrong.

No sooner had we stepped onto the road with our arms outstretched than a car stopped—the very first car that approached us. The driver was a lady heading for work. Her place of employment was located past the Banias Nature Reserve, and she was willing to give us a ride.

Along the way, we passed through a village named Mas'ada, a Syrian village that had been captured in 1967. The residents are called *Druze*. Their religion is neither Jewish nor Muslim nor Christian, but a strange fusion that also includes many Eastern religions. Most of these folks still consider themselves to be Syrian, although up to 10 percent have taken on Israeli citizenship. Israel holds the governing rule of the town of thirty-five hundred. According to our driver that morning, the Druze are loyal to whoever controls them. Mainly peace loving, they will join the Israeli military or would quickly revert to Syrian allegiance, should control of their town ever change.

Our kind driver delivered us to the front entrance of the nature reserve. The park didn't open until 8:00 a.m., and we were there by 7:30.

Since we had a half hour before we would be admitted, we decided to walk beyond the park, along the main highway. As we walked, we passed numerous signs warning us not to leave the road; the surrounding area is still littered with mines from the 1967 war.

When we topped a crest in the road, the town of Dan stretched out ahead of us. The Old Testament tells us that it was here that King Jeroboam built the "high places" where the children of Israel worshipped false gods. This led to the worship of Baal and angered God greatly. Later, when Greek culture held a prominent influence in the area, the Greek fertility gods were also worshipped.

A small side road led away from the main highway, and we

wished to discover what lay beyond. But a high metal fence stopped us from any further exploration in that direction. What lay beyond the fence was the Lebanon border.

Across the road lay another mystery. A driveway led away from the road, but a fence and gate prohibited us from entering there, too. A posted sign told us it was a mosque and warned any wanderers wandering about that no praying would be permitted.

We leaned up against the gate and prayed.

If that sign warning us not to pray had not been there, we probably would not have thought of doing so. Perhaps we need more signs like that to wake up slumbering prayer warriors?

We returned to the entrance of the park and were the first two admitted that day. Soon a stream of tourist buses also began to arrive.

All of these folks were coming to Caesarea Philippi, as Jesus had done one day with His disciples. I doubt, though, that Jesus took a bus. He probably walked the twenty-five miles from Capernaum to Caesarea Philippi.

. . .

Banias Nature Reserve is at the base of Mt. Hermon, Israel's tallest mountain. From here, the Jordan River begins its flow south toward the Sea of Galilee. The largest waterfall in Israel is located in this reserve.

Because of the abundant source of water, this became a hub of religious rites. In Old Testament times, this area was known as Baal Hermon or Baal Gad. During the time the Romans ruled the territory, numerous pagan temples were also built here.

The Greek influence is possibly the most prominent of the pagan worship influences. The temple of the Greek god Pan is a central attraction for tourists. Pan was the god of nature, mountains, meadows, forests, and of hunting. This area is beautiful, with forests, lush green flora, and many waterfalls. The landscape is a strong contrast to most of Israel, and it's easy to see why worshippers would think this the perfect spot for Pan's temple.

Somehow, Pan's job description also included being the god of shepherds. The mythological creature is depicted as half goat and half man. Finally, he was also considered the god of both fertility and fright; the word *panic* derives from his name. Caesarea Philippi was named Panias when it was under Greek rule. The current name, Banias, derives from that.

A large cave at the base of a cliff became the focal point of Pan worship. Around the mouth of the cave, recesses carved into the rock face hold statues of other creatures of Greek mythology. The niches also contain the names of folks who donated large sums of money to make this temple area possible. It seems to me that not much has changed since the days of Pan worship. Today, many of our temples of higher learning bear inscriptions of names of donors who have given of their resources so our youth can be taught pagan beliefs.

A spring flowed from the cave, and worshippers thought that this was an entrance to the underworld where their gods and goddesses lived. The belief was that Pan spent his winter months beneath this cave (much like many of us northerners spend the winter in Florida), and returned to the woods and mountains in the spring. To coax him back so that new life could begin again, worshippers engaged in rites too horrible and degraded to describe here. In addition, human sacrifices were tossed into the waters of the spring. If the gods were satisfied with the sacrifice, the body vanished without a trace. If the gods were grumpy that day and for some reason found the human a defective and unworthy sacrifice, blood would bubble to the surface of the water.

Either way, the man, woman, or child was drowned and gone.

Is it any wonder that this place became known as the Gates of Hell?

In Matthew 16, verse 13, we read that Jesus took His disciples to the region of Caesarea Philippi. One can almost imagine their consternation when they heard that Jesus was taking them to this area. We are not told whether Jesus visited this specific cave, but surely the wicked pagan rites of the area would have been mentioned in conversation among themselves.

"Why are we going to that town?"

"I've heard about what goes on at their temples."

"Can you believe He's actually taking us *there?*"

No self-respecting Jew would ever consider going to Caesarea Philippi. That's akin to us modern-day Christians going where sinners reside, places where no self-respecting Christian would want to be seen. What would the folks back home say if they discovered you took your Christian self to the local Gates of Hell?

Jesus did, though.

So perhaps we should consider storming the Gates of Hell, too. Or are we too timid or self-righteous to do that?

Imagine the contrast the disciples were seeing. From the ultra-strict synagogues of Jewish tradition, Jesus and His disciples walked a short two days (about twenty-five miles) to the center of pagan depravity.

Why would Jesus have brought them here? Craig and I pondered the question as we stood at the grotto called *the Temple of Pan.*

"Possibly," said Craig, "it was to show the disciples to what levels of evil mankind can sink."

Or perhaps Jesus wished to show the disciples and us that He had come to this earth to overcome such evil.

It was in the Caesarea Philippi area that Jesus asked the disciples a very pointed question.

"Who do people say the Son of Man is?"

"Well, some think you are John the Baptist, come back to life," said one of the disciples.

"Elijah," said another.

"Jeremiah, or perhaps one of the prophets," said a third.

"But what about you? Who do you say that I am?" persisted Jesus.

"You are the Christ, the Son of the living God!" declared Peter.

Jesus asks the same question of you and me. Our answer will determine our destiny and where we live forever, after we finish with this life.

What about you? Who do you say that I am?

At times I may write as if I make light of some spiritual applications or Biblical events. It's my attempt as a writer to bring humor to situations.

This, however, is not one of those times. This is the most important question you, my reader, will ever answer. I would encourage you to pause right here and contemplate your answer.

It's not enough to believe *about* Jesus. Many folks believe Jesus existed but don't actually believe He is the Christ, the Son of the living God.

It took much wandering and many journeys for me, your humble writer, to finally say with confidence that I believe Jesus is who He says He is.

Peter said what he had come to believe. And he said it with confidence.

"You are the Messiah, the Son of the living God."

Jesus replied, "You, Peter, are the rock upon which I will build my church, and the Gates of Hell will not overcome it."

Was Jesus speaking about the Gates of Hell there in Caesarea Philippi and reminding the disciples that He could overcome even such evil? Or was He saying that hell could not withstand the church He was bringing to fruition?

Do you suppose Jesus actually intended for His church—that is, *you and I*—to press forward against the Gates of Hell in our own neighborhoods and communities?

Onward, Christian soldiers. March to war!

. . .

Not long after Jesus had taken his disciples to Caesarea Philippi, He determined to take that final journey to Jerusalem. We also were determined to set our bodies toward Jerusalem following our visit to the nature reserve.

There was a distinct difference in our journeys, however. Before Jesus departed for Jerusalem, He would have His body transfigured; His face shone like the sun, and His clothes became white as snow.

My body didn't shine like the sun, but my mind had a transfiguration of sorts. I suppose I could make a case that my body did as well.

A trail winds its way through the Banias Reserve and leads to a beautiful waterfall. From that falls, the Jordan River flows onward and meanders its way to the Sea of Galilee.

One of my goals for my time in Israel was to be baptized in the Jordan River. It's something most Christian tourists do. Jesus thought it was important to be baptized; He traveled to the Jordan specifically for that. I wanted the experience, too, and now I was standing at the river.

Why not now, right here?

The 13ᵗʰ Disciple

However, this would not be quite the experience Jesus had. He was baptized on the south side of the Sea of Galilee, where the waters of the Jordan are a good bit warmer than in the north. The waters in the Banias Reserve are recent runoff from snows on Mount Hermon.

Another deterrent to my being immersed in Jordan's rushing waters was that I could only be immersed to a depth of about five inches—the water was only slightly above my ankles. At that point, the Jordan is only then being born and not yet deep enough for a good dunking. I suppose I could have had my ankles sprinkled. That way both ends of my body would have been covered by a sprinkling baptism.

Craig suggested another form of baptism, a baptism utilized by his group on a previous trip to Israel. I agreed.

I found a rock on the riverbank and sat down, took off my shoes and socks, and dropped my feet into Jordan Creek. Beside me, Craig did the same.

We dipped our hands into the water and poured it over our eyes as Craig prayed for good sight. Then the water fell over our ears, as he prayed for them to be opened to hear what God wants us to hear. Our tongue was baptized to speak words of kindness to others and to praise God. Body part by body part, we baptized. Our feet to walk uprightly, our stomachs to enjoy good health. We asked for a baptism of our minds that would bring good thoughts and wisdom.

Wouldn't it be a good idea for parents to baptize their young children in this way, to cover all of their body parts in prayer as they go to school or play?

Lastly, we grasped a handful of water and slowly let it flow back into the river that leads to the Sea of Galilee as we prayed over this book that was then no more than an intention in my mind.

If you're reading this book now and finding a closer connection to Jesus of Nazareth, then I believe it is due to that baptismal service.

CHAPTER 18

Road to Jerusalem

It was Election Day in the U.S. The baptismal service ended about 10:00 a.m. We had only one possible connection that could get us to Jerusalem in time for me to watch the election results, and at 1:00 p.m., that connection would depart from the bus stop in Odem.

It was all a bit more complicated than catching one bus. The bus from Odem went to Kiryat Shmona, a town only twenty-four miles from Odem. In that town, we would catch a bus to Tel Aviv and there connect to yet a final bus to Jerusalem. One and only one bus went from Kiryat Shmona to Tel Aviv, and it left at 4:00 p.m.

But if we could get back to Odem in time for the one o'clock bus, we would have smooth sailing. Even if we were on the slowest bus in the world, it could surely get to Kiryat Shmona—just twenty-four miles away, remember—in three hours.

The first goal was to return to Odem. We had to catch that first bus.

The 13th Disciple

As we exited the Banias Reserve, we approached several coaches lined up in the parking area and inquired about the possibility of catching a ride.

That idea went over like the proverbial lead balloon. Furthermore, all the drivers seemed to be heading in the opposite direction. (Unfortunately, we had told them where we wanted to go.) I would venture a guess there are bus-line regulations prohibiting hitchhikers, anyway.

We entered the roadway and extended our arms in anticipation of a ride.

We extended and anticipated for quite some time and a few miles.

It was a hot day, and we were walking uphill. Alongside the road, several Muslim ladies were atop ladders, picking olives in a grove. They seemed to be oblivious to the two hikers on the roadway.

Several times, our spirits jumped as a vehicle seemed to slow down. However, most of the time it was only vehicles downshifting as they traversed the hill.

Finally, a utility van slowed to a stop. A Muslim man was driving and invited us in. He had also picked up two hitchhiking Israeli soldiers on leave. The two soldiers had suggested the driver stop and pick us up. Oh, what a relief.

The driver could only take us as far as the Druze town of Mas'ada, but that would at least get us to within six miles of Odem.

After being dropped off at the far edge of Mas'ada, we started the next leg of our journey. A herd of goats, numbering at least a hundred, was plodding alongside the highway. A goat herder and his dog followed, attempting to keep the goats off the highway. Many of the animals did trot onto the roadway, possibly seeking sustenance, since the ground they walked on was merely rocks and dirt. The larger goats could reach up and snag a few leaves from low-hanging tree branches.

The tinkling of the goats' bells surrounded us as we walked on, arms outstretched.

A vehicle slowed down and stopped. The young man behind the wheel offered to take us as far as the road leading to Odem.

Again, relief. From that drop-off point, we knew we had time to walk back to the hostel, clean up, and catch that one o'clock bus.

. . .

The bus stopped directly in front of our hostel at the one o'clock hour.

We boarded and celebrated. We were on the bus! Smooth sailing to Jerusalem!

The first inkling I had that something was amiss was when we hit the main highway where we had first attempted to hitchhike with a dog in tow. There, the driver did not turn toward Kiryat Schmona, but went in the opposite direction.

Perhaps this bus takes a longer loop and makes several stops, I thought, still optimistic.

We were taken on a circuitous tour of the Golan Heights. I am sure we saw almost every small outpost and community in the Golan. It was fascinating for a while, seeing the daily activities of these settlements from my bus window. The bus stopped often, and newcomers would enter with shouts of greeting to other passengers they knew. In the town of Dan, the driver maneuvered through streets I would have had difficulty navigating with a VW Beetle. The bus kept stopping, and the clock kept moving toward that four o'clock hour.

Finally, we reached the outskirts of Kiryat Shmona. Still, we stopped. At one stop, an Israeli soldier took the seat in front of us. We exchanged pleasantries and asked him for information about the central bus terminal where we hoped to connect with our next bus.

"Oh, there are two more stops before you arrive there," he told us.

That would make a total of seventeen stops and almost three hours to travel twenty-four miles. And, the soldier assured us, the bus for Tel Aviv did leave *promptly* at four.

Arriving at the terminal, the young soldier directed us to the slot where we would find the bus for Tel Aviv.

We were so close, so close.

And then, Craig decided this would be a place he could find a restroom without the threat of land mines exploding.

I asked the driver how much time we had before departure. He said he was leaving in two minutes.

I had one chance and one chance only to watch that election, and I wasn't about to miss it. I yelled at Craig to either get on the bus or be left behind.

The door shut—behind us both—and we were off toward Tel Aviv.

Fortunately, this three-and-a-half-hour ride didn't include seventeen stops. The bus did make one stop midway to Tel Aviv to give the driver and passengers an opportunity to get out and stretch our legs for twenty minutes. This rest stop included a gas station, café, and some good old home cooking—McDonald's.

I took this opportunity to ask our driver about connecting with the next bus that would take us to Jerusalem. It would be bus number 480, he told me, and would be located a short distance from where we would be unloading in Tel Aviv.

As we resumed the drive, it was interesting to sit by the window and watch the road signs flashing by. Some I had seen while traveling at a much slower pace just a few days before. The Tiberius exit presented itself, and a half hour later, the sign for Nazareth flashed by. Craig and I had walked that distance in three days, and I'm guessing Jesus probably did it in better time than we had.

At Haifa, on the coast, we turned south and followed the coastline to Tel Aviv.

Darkness had descended upon the city when we arrived and were dumped on the street. No buses were in sight.

After taking several fruitless jaunts down wrong streets, we spied a lot where buses were parked side-by-side in long lines stretching across the lot. It was the birthplace of buses.

We were either blessed or just incredibly fortunate that I recalled it was bus number 480 we wanted, and 480 was the very first bus we came upon.

I inquired of the driver how much time we had until he departed for Jerusalem. He replied, "You have no time. Get on, so I can close the door."

We did, and he did.

At 8:00 p.m., we arrived in Jerusalem.

Had it really been only thirteen hours before that Craig and I had our first hitchhike? Three hitches and three bus rides later and lots of living in between brought us to our destination, the City of David. I imagine in all of our lives we can look back and reflect on special days that have held more living than others. This day will forever be at the top of my list.

We had arrived in Jerusalem in the evening, just as Jesus had arrived for the Feast of Unleavened Bread. He would have arrived via the Pilgrim Road on a donkey colt, and we had arrived via Jaffa Street on a bus.

The 13ᵗʰ Disciple

. . .

In Luke 9, Luke wrote that when the time drew near for Jesus to ascend to Heaven, He "resolutely set out for Jerusalem." The definition of *resolute* is *purposeful, determined,* and *unwavering.* Other synonyms are *unshakable* and *unhesitating.*

That also seems like a good description of people who have made the choice to follow Jesus.

It appears that Jesus chose the shortest route to Jerusalem, straight through Samaria. He sent messengers ahead to make preparations. However, He was not welcome in one Samaritan village and was refused their hospitality.

Angered, James and John wanted to command fire to come down from Heaven to destroy that village. I can imagine Jesus looking at the brothers and saying, "Really, fellows, haven't I taught you better?"

Instead of stopping in the hostile town, Jesus turned eastward, crossed the Jordan, and came through Judea. This meant Jesus approached Jerusalem by way of Jericho. How fortunate for several folks we know who lived in that town.

One was Zacchaeus. He was another one of those "scum," those tax collectors who were automatically labeled "sinners." He was the chief tax collector in Jericho and very rich. But he had heard about this Jesus, and he wanted to know more about the man.

You know the story. He couldn't see, so he climbed the sycamore tree. (Hear that children's song in your head?)

This story reminds me of something James, the brother of Jesus, wrote years later: "Draw close to God, and he will draw close to you" (James 4:8). We may, as humans, wonder how we can ever hope to draw close to the Almighty Creator, but this verse reassures us that God recognizes those who have the desire to know Him, and He comes to us.

Just so with Zacchaeus. Jesus spotted him up in that tree, and He came to Zacchaeus, even called him by name. "I'm going to stay with you tonight," Jesus called up into the branches. Of course, that riled up more than a few holier-than-thou people in the crowd. *There goes Jesus again, gone to be the guest of a notorious sinner.*

And again, this sinner decided to follow Jesus.

Another resident of Jericho was one man known as Blind Bartimaeus. He sat along the road and begged. He was at the mercy of those who passed by, depending on the compassion of others.

Then he heard a large crowd approaching, and he caught the name of Jesus of Nazareth. Bart had heard about this man!

He started yelling for Jesus' attention. "Son of David, have mercy on me!"

Somehow, above the noise and din of the crowd, Jesus heard that plea for mercy.

"What do you want?" Jesus asked.

"I want to see."

Bartimaeus had faith that Jesus could heal him.

"Your faith has healed you," responded Jesus. And Bart could see.

I believe that's how easy it is for Jesus to heal sin in our lives. We often make it too difficult for folks to unload their baggage.

"What do you want?" asks Jesus.

"I want to be free of this guilt and bondage."

"You are free. Your faith has healed you," Jesus will say.

. . .

Approaching Jerusalem, Jesus entered Bethany, not far from the Mount of Olives. Jesus' friends, Mary and Martha and Lazarus, lived in this town.

Jesus sent two disciples a little farther ahead to the village of Bethphage with instructions to fetch a donkey's colt that they would find tied up at a certain place. There is some debate whether Jesus had previously made arrangements for that colt or whether Jesus, in His divinity, knew that it was there and that the owner would lend it to Him.

Of more interest to me is the fact that this colt might very well have been born in a barn. The colt had never been ridden before. A wild colt would have tossed off any rider. However, this colt was docile. I'm also aware, though, that if Jesus could command the waves of the sea to calm at his word or dead Lazarus to come out of a tomb, then Jesus could certainly tame a wild colt, as well.

As Jesus rode into Jerusalem, folks spread cloaks and branches on the road, welcoming Him. It created quite an uproar; the people were hailing Him as a King sent from God, and the Pharisees were quite distressed.

Jesus immediately went to the Temple. Since it was late in the evening, He just looked around and surveyed what was going on. Then He returned to Bethany with the twelve disciples, with plans to return the next day. I assume He stayed at Mary and Martha's that night. I believe that in Jesus' humanity some emotions were already riled up by what He had observed in the Temple.

The next morning, Jesus and His friends left Bethany to go back to the Temple. Maybe Martha wasn't up yet when they left, because breakfast must have been slim pickings that morning. Mark 11:12 states that Jesus was hungry. He spotted a fig tree with leaves aflutter. However, this tree was fruitless.

Although my knowledge of fig trees is limited, I do know that a fig tree can produce several crops per year. Often, fruit was available up to ten months of the year. In early spring, the fig was a green color and would be growing even before the leaves unfurled. Therefore, when Jesus and the disciples saw the tree in full leaf, they probably assumed there was fruit available. But there was nothing.

If Jesus could turn water into wine, why not just command figs to present themselves? This story obviously has symbolic meaning which, for many of us, is unclear.

Some say that Jesus' cursing of the fig tree was symbolic of the judgment and rejection of Israel. Still others think it might represent so-called Christians festooned only with leaves—bearing a pretense of religion with no actual fruit. Another interpretation points to the significance of the nearby town of Bethphage—the location of the Sanhedrin council that made many decisions about the Jewish law. The meaning of *Bethphage* is *House of unripe figs*. The Jewish law was fruitless; only Jesus could fulfill what the law was meant to do in making the people of God holy. And yet one more viewpoint is that the fruit eaten by Adam and Eve was a fig, and in withering the fig tree, Jesus points to the outcome of His death—breaking the power of sin that held mankind in slavery.

All of those commentaries might have merit, but could it just possibly be that Jesus was under great duress and was frustrated by the lack of fruit and showed his frustration? We so often tend to think only of the divinity of Jesus, and we forget that He had to deal with the whole gamut of emotions we also must deal with.

He was about to exhibit another emotion: anger. I wonder if, during the previous evening, He saw how the Temple area was being commercialized. "Zeal for God's house consumed Him," says the Scripture. Jesus went on more than a rant; He instigated a purge, upsetting the tables of moneychangers and the benches of those selling doves. "Get these out of here!"

I like that display of emotions. I think Christians should display more Godly anger at situations around us. But we are far too pious to do that.

Jesus was now setting in motion events that would get Him killed within the week. You do not mess with the authorities making money.

. . .

Jesus and I had both arrived in Jerusalem, although by different routes and different modes of transportation. Jesus went off to the Temple on His first evening in town. I planned to park myself in front of a television and watch the election returns in the U.S.A.

We descended to the street, officially ending our marathon bus trip. Our next goal was to find the Abraham Hostel Jerusalem.

Craig had assured me that this Jerusalem hostel "should" have adequate rooms available and that we "shouldn't" need a reservation. And I was trusting that the amenities there would be similar to the Abraham Hostel in Tel Aviv, where we had stayed when we first arrived in Israel. At the top of my list of desired amenities was a television available in each room. Or, at least, somewhere on the property.

We asked for directions to the hostel, and I realized we had entered a landscape of wonderment. Jewish men, especially, stood out in the crowd, with their odd garb. Many were dressed in black and white, with black hats atop their heads. An Amish man from Ohio could have gone unnoticed in this crowd.

The Abraham Hostel was surprisingly abuzz with activity for the late evening hour. I scanned the surroundings as we entered, hoping to discover a working television in some corner, just in case our room was not furnished with one. As we presented ourselves at the main desk, I asked immediately if there were televisions in the rooms.

No. No television. And we're sorry, but we also don't have any rooms available.

No room in the inn.

Lots of young folks were arriving in Jerusalem that night, the young man at the desk told us. These arrivals had had the foresight to make a reservation. We were invited to wait and see if any reservations would be canceled.

We waited. But not patiently.

At least, I was not patient. Back in the United States, votes were being cast. Things were happening. States were turning red and blue. People were celebrating or despairing.

And I was missing it. I felt panic start to set in.

I kept checking with the front desk to see if anyone had canceled. I soon got the distinct impression that the young man thought that the five long minutes I waited between trips to his desk were not long enough. He finally took the time to call several other places to inquire about vacancies for us. I don't think he was being helpful; at that point, I think he just wanted us out of his lobby.

We needed a Plan B, and we needed it quick. All around Jerusalem, rooms were selling out at an alarming rate. I could feel opportunity slipping away from us.

Craig asked for the use of my iPad and went to work. Through a travel website, he snagged a room at another hostel several blocks away.

Back to the streets we went. After missing and searching for the entry to the building, we finally checked in at the Stay Inn, a renovated youth hostel on the third floor of an otherwise nondescript building.

I know what you're thinking. You're wondering why two sixty-plus-year-old men stay in youth hostels. I define myself as still quite youthful and I hope useful, so I believe I fit right in. And you'll have to admit, compared to Methuselah we are rather spring chickens. An additional qualification would be that we had walked more miles than any of the youth gathered there.

Some might think God doesn't trouble Himself with the small details in our lives. Surely God had more important things to do that night than direct us to a hostel with televisions in the rooms. But He did just that. Not only was a television awaiting us, but it was a large-screen color television that greeted me as I walked into a newly remodeled room.

All the American news shows were available to us. Live and direct from Election Central USA, the results came in as we watched from the other side of the Atlantic.

Before getting too deeply engrossed with the election coverage, we needed food. It had been a long and exciting day of living with little sustenance. En route to our dwelling place, we had passed several open-air food shops that were open late. One such enterprise had promised delicious falafels, and we decided to return there.

It is possible that in their prime these falafels could have had a slightly favorable taste. However, that would have been about twelve hours before we stood at the counter.

I assumed I was getting a meatball sandwich. A variety of vegetables were still lazing about at the bottom of nearly empty containers. Craig and I were the cleanup crew. The proprietor dumped a large serving of pretend meatballs into pita bread and stuffed every crack and crevasse with tomatoes, pickles, lettuce, and a variety of mystery foods. It could be that he had swept up the floor and our pitas were just convenient containers to dispose of the sweepings.

Back up in our room at Election Central Jerusalem, I launched into my pita burger.

"These meatballs are horrid," I told Craig.

"Those aren't meatballs. Those are mashed up chickpeas," he told me.

The aforementioned vegetable had suffered a devastating crushing in some type of blender and was ignobly formed into a dough ball, dropped into a cooker of hot oil, and brought forth as an orb masquerading as a meatball. These were falafels, although those in my pita that evening did not deserve the name. As a former restaurant manager, I have always believed any food can be made palatable with enough sugar or butter. I had finally found the one food item that debunked that notion.

I started my marathon election night. Israel was seven hours behind American television viewers, so it was the middle of the night in Israel when the polls closed and returns came in.

When the election results were announced, the outcome weighed heavily on the minds of many devastated newsmakers and voters across the fruited plains.

And one partly eaten stuffed pita weighed heavily in my stomach.

. . .

The U.S. news broadcasts filled our hostel room and I was entertained by the seismic aftershock until ten o'clock the following morning. A new president had been elected. The sun had come up, after all, and the solar system and all of God's creation still functioned as it was intended to. That is, all was functioning except one segment of humanity. That segment had been thrown off kilter more than a bit.

Oh, well, I doubted that God was surprised by the outcome. I didn't plan to spend any time worrying about the results of the election. I had been prepared to accept either candidate as our new president, believing that God is, indeed, still on the throne.

Out on the streets of Jerusalem, there was considerable talk about the night's events in the States. Some believed, as we had heard from many of the soldiers we spoke with, that the losing candidate might have better served Israel's security. Others with a less liberal bent believed the new president would be more open to the protection of Israel's borders.

Election Day was over. I was in Jerusalem, where God had already done so many miracles on Israel's behalf. It was time to discover for myself what wonders this city held.

CHAPTER 19

The Old City

Modern-day Jerusalem is a far cry from the city King David made his capital. Its population was almost nine hundred thousand in 2015, and it covers 48.3 square miles. Within that metropolis is the walled area known as the Old City, which was the entirety of Jerusalem back in the sixteenth century when the massive stone walls were built to defend against enemies. The Old City covers a mere one-third square mile, which would be about 224 acres.

Within the Old City are sites regarded as holy by the three main religions in Jerusalem—Islam, Christianity, and Judaism. The Old City is divided into quarters, although they are not equal in size. The Muslim quarter is the largest, located in the northeast portion of the Old City. The Jewish quarter occupies the southeast section, the Armenian Christian section is in the southwest and is the smallest in size, and the Christian quarter is in the northwest. The population within the Old City's walls is about thirty-five thousand.

Those neighborhoods within the ancient walls create a

microcosm of the greater Jerusalem and, further, the Middle East. Three major religions live side by side, their lives intermingling and overlapping, their lifestyles and beliefs vastly different, friction arising at times, and outright conflict and violence always close to the surface as all three make claims and assert their presence and "rights" and "rightness." To complicate matters even further, conflict also exists within the three religions: Orthodox and ultra-Orthodox Jew versus liberal Jew, Hamas versus Fatah Palestinians, conservative versus liberal Christian. The city from which Jesus will someday lead the world to peace is anything but peaceful.

Nothing in my own experience compares to this. I grew up in a community somewhat insulated from the rest of the world. The population of my county is fairly homogeneous, a majority of the churches hold similar beliefs even though we're of different denominations, and we are citizens of one government (although we can certainly have heated political debates at times).

The walls of the Old City were about a fifteen-minute walk from our hostel. Eight magnificent gates were built into the thick walls. Going through some of the ancient gates is almost like walking through a short tunnel. We would enter Old Jerusalem by the Jaffa gate, ushering us in between the Christian quarter and the Armenian quarter. This gate was used by pilgrims coming to Jerusalem by the road from Jaffa Port, a town on the Mediterranean Sea just south of Tel Aviv. You might also remember that Jonah tried to sail away from God by catching a boat in Jaffa.

As we approached the Jaffa Gate, I could easily understand what upset Jesus as He walked to the Temple. I wonder what He thinks today about the scene. Vendors were everywhere, selling all types of goods. Food, cards, clothes—any and every imaginable item with any faint representation of Jewish life was carved, molded, sewn, or otherwise made into an object to be sold.

The moneychangers today no longer sit at tables exchanging currency. They stand silently, embedded in walls here and there, their visages made of metal and plastic. All one needs is a card to insert into the metal mouth, and at the push of buttons, the moneychanger returns American greenbacks.

. . .

One of the first places I wanted to visit was the Western Wall. It has sometimes been known as the Wailing Wall, although that's not a term Jewish people would use.

The short section of the stone wall, about 187 feet long and 62 feet high, is a remnant of the ancient wall that surrounded the Temple courtyard. The Western Wall is actually just a small section of a much longer wall that served as a retaining wall encircling the steep hill— the mountaintop, actually. The two previous Temples were built on top of Mount Moriah, the highest point in Old Jerusalem. It was on Mount Moriah that Abraham prepared to sacrifice his son; it was the site of Solomon's Temple, and some say it might even have been the place where God first breathed into dust and created a living soul.

Let's take a brief survey of the history of the Temple. The first Temple, built by King Solomon, was destroyed by the Babylonians in 586 B.C. When the Jewish exiles returned seventy years later, the Temple was rebuilt and a King Herod made it a place of great splendor. That was the Temple still standing in Jerusalem when Jesus visited. That second Temple was destroyed by the Romans seventy years after the birth of Jesus, and the ruins were left untouched until the Muslims took control of Jerusalem in 638 A.D. By the year 1033 A.D., the Muslims had built both a mosque and the Dome of the

Rock, a shrine for pilgrims, on the area called *the Temple Mount.*
That changed again when the Crusades put the Temple Mount in
Christian hands. The Dome of the Rock was then used as a church
until 1187 A.D., when it was taken again by the Muslims.

That's a simplified summary, but you begin to see the ongoing
struggle for control, not only in Jerusalem but all of Israel.

For Jews, this small section of the retaining wall became a
pilgrimage destination, since it was the only surviving part of their
Temple. On the other side of that wall is the spot where the Holy
of Holies, the most sacred part of the Temple, once stood. It is now
lying under Muslim control. The Jews came to pray at the wall, and,
one can imagine, to mourn. I'm sure that's how the term "Wailing
Wall" emerged, but it's actually considered a derogatory term by
Jews.

That spot where the Holy of Holies was believed to have been
is marked by the Foundation Stone, an area of bare bedrock. The
Foundation Stone lies inside the Dome of the Rock. Some people
believe that the Ark of the Covenant is also buried somewhere under
the Temple Mount, covered over with layers and layers of historical
debris.

Around the thirty-seven-acre Temple Mount, the city has grown
up, and now homes and other structures surround the Wall and
create a plaza, an open concourse where people still come for prayers,
readings, and ceremonial events—and tourists come to watch.

Admittance to the plaza is limited to two entrances, and at both,
people must walk through metal detectors. A high, covered walkway
crosses above one end of the plaza, an access point to the Temple
Mount above the wall. Jews and tourists are allowed to enter the
Temple Mount, but non-Muslim prayers are not permitted. On
Friday evenings, when Jews are praying at the Wall, no Muslim

under forty-five years of age may be on the Mount—another security measure, since rocks and trash have been thrown down to harass those praying. Longer ago, Muslims even used the Wall as a garbage dump, to humiliate any Jew praying below.

In 1949, Jordan (who then controlled the Temple Mount) signed an agreement allowing Jews the right to visit the Western Wall. The words on paper never became reality, and not one Jew was permitted to visit. That all changed in 1967, when Israel was attacked by her neighbors. After the dust settled from the Six-Day War, the neighbors no longer controlled who could pray at the Wall. It was in Jewish hands again, where it is to this day. At the conclusion of that short war, Defense Minister Moshe Dayan was one of the first to pray at the Western Wall.

. . .

Craig believed he knew the correct street that would lead us to the Western Wall. The Old City of Jerusalem is a maze of alleys and side streets, and one can easily get confused.

The Western Wall is actually directly *east* of the Jaffa Gate. If you're trying to picture Old Jerusalem, Jaffa Gate is on the western side, and the Temple Mount is on the eastern side, between the Jewish quarter and the Muslim quarter. The wall is called the *Western* Wall because it is on the west side of the Temple Mount.

First, though, Craig wanted me to see the golden menorah. We could not miss it. It stood in a display case at the top of the stairs that led down to the Western Wall prayer plaza.

The Temple Institute, an organization based in the Jewish quarter of the Old City, is a nonprofit group dedicated to the building of the *third* Temple on Mount Moriah. There is, of course, a huge problem to be solved before that construction can take place on the Temple Mount: Muslim real estate sits atop that site.

Some Biblical scholars believe that the Temple will not be rebuilt until Jesus returns to the earth. Others believe that the Temple must be ready when the Prince of Peace does come to reign. If the Temple is not ready for Him and the Muslim sites are the holdup and need to be removed, I'm sure Jesus is up for the task.

Although they cannot yet start building the Temple itself, Temple Institute scholars are meticulously creating sacred vessels and vestments that will be used in the Temple. After years of research and study, they are producing detailed blueprints and patterns according to God's instructions in the Old Testament and historical records. These are not simply models of what, for example, the altar might have been like. These are designed and created by expert craftsmen for use in the new Temple that will someday be constructed. A shovel and a fork, a wine decanter and a container for grain offerings, an oil pitcher, a golden flask for olive oil, and an incense chalice are among the smaller items already completed. Larger items prepared and ready for service in the new Temple include the incense altar, the table of the showbread, the golden menorah, and the Ark of the Covenant. The vestments of the high priest are also finished and ready for the future high priest to wear.

The golden menorah weighs a total of one thousand pounds and contains one hundred pounds of pure gold. Its display case at the top of the stairs looks across the Western Wall plaza to the Temple Mount, as though it is waiting to be moved there.

We followed the stairs downward to the plaza and endured a process Jesus never underwent: a security check. Every visitor must go through a screening much like we go through at an airport security checkpoint.

The Old City

It was a Wednesday morning, and not many people were at the Wall. The huge hewn-limestone blocks making up the wall are at least four feet high and even longer. Those stones were there when Jesus walked through this town. A flight of stone stairs going up to the Temple Mount are now closed off, but Jesus' sandals very likely raised the dust on those stairs.

Men are required to wear a head covering when approaching the wall. A yarmulke, a small cap fitting firmly over the top of the head, is normally worn. Donning one of the paper yarmulkes provided for visitors, I went to the Wall and rested my head against the ancient stone for my own time of prayer.

A tradition has grown up. People write prayers and petitions on slips of paper and leave them in any crack or crevice they can find in and between the stones. I had written my own prayer to leave there—a prayer for our country and our new president.

. . .

Outside the walls of Old Jerusalem, modern city streets and sidewalks were busy with urban traffic. Craig and I went back outside the walls to stroll around the perimeter of the Old City. We stopped on the walkway in front of the Golden Gate and gazed across a ravine to the opposite hillside.

It's difficult for me to describe the feelings stirred when I stood and looked across the Kidron Valley to a garden that we know was a place Jesus frequented. He would have walked through that garden and up over the Mount of Olives, walking to Bethany and the house of His friends, Mary, Martha, and Lazarus.

In ancient times, olive trees covered the slopes of the Mount of Olives. Now, the slope of the hill is filled with thousands of tombs.

The gravesites are not marked with stones such as we would use in the States. Instead, boxes roughly the size and shape of a coffin sit atop each grave.

"That hillside," Craig remarked, "is the most expensive real estate in the world." Prominent and wealthy Jewish people are buried there; purchasing a burial plot in that location requires lots and lots of shekels. Jewish belief is that when the Messiah does come, those who are "sleeping" on the hillside of the Mount of Olives will be the first to come out of their graves and witness His coming.

Behind us was the towering Golden Gate, also at times referred to as the *Gate of Mercy.* Here, the wall of the Old City is also the eastern wall of the Temple Mount, so this gate leads directly into the area where the Temple stood in Jesus' time. It is believed that this is the gate Jesus entered on Palm Sunday.

The Jews believe that the Messiah will enter the city through this gate when He comes. He *has* come. And when I consider how Jesus fulfilled all the prophecies of the promised Messiah, it's difficult for me to comprehend why the Jews are still waiting for Him to appear.

When the Muslims conquered Jerusalem in the sixteenth century, they sealed this gate, and it has not been opened in the centuries since. The slope below the gate was then used as Muslim burial grounds.

We stood in front of the gate, looking out over the Muslim graves below us and across the Kidron Valley to the Jewish graveyard. Somewhere on the slope of the Mount of Olives there is also a Christian cemetery. All three religions expect this gate to be an important place in the day that Jesus appears on earth to deliver and judge.

As we gazed at the Mount of Olives, we were oblivious to two men sneaking up behind us. When they grabbed us, we were stunned, and for a few brief seconds we were convinced we were either being arrested or robbed.

However, much to our surprise (and relief), the two were Lee and Mike, the men we had met while having supper back in Nazareth. In the teeming masses assembled in Jerusalem that day, we had somehow again crossed paths, and we all agreed to join up later that evening for a meal.

. . .

The first Biblical mention of the Mount of Olives is in 2 Samuel 15:30 when we see David weeping as he walks up the road to the Mount. He has his head covered and is barefoot, signs of mourning. He is leaving the city because his son Absalom has gathered forces and is entering Jerusalem to take the throne away from David.

Another of David's sons, though, would eventually inherit the throne. King Solomon was known for his wealth, success in war, and wisdom. He seemed to have it all. But, Scripture accounts say, he loved many women, and many of them were wives he found among pagan nations. To please them, Solomon built altars and places of worship for their foreign gods on top of the Mount of Olives. This provoked God's anger and was the reason God split the kingdom in two.

Years later, King Josiah had a house cleaning and demolished the altars, beating them into dust and disposing of the dust in the Kidron brook. He also cut down all the olive trees and replaced them with the bones of men. You can read all about it in 2 Kings 23:12-14.

The Mount of Olives also plays a prominent part in prophecies about the future. Zechariah 14:1-11 gives details. If you were paying attention as you read this book, you'll recall that when Jesus returns, this mountain will be split in two, presenting an escape route for the folks remaining in Jerusalem. Today, at the top of the Mount of Olives, there is a hotel fronted with seven arches. (Yes, it's called the *Hotel 7 Arches*.) When this hotel was being built, a major fault that runs under the construction site was discovered. Prophecies that were puzzling to me at one time were beginning to become real.

It is my assumption that at some point after the splitting of the Mount of Olives, Jesus will not be deterred by the Muslim cemetery, will remove the impediment of the sealed Golden Gate, and will bring peace to Jerusalem once and for all. Greater minds than mine can grapple with the sequence of events.

Our crossing of the Kidron Valley required skill not necessary for Jesus or His disciples. We needed to dodge through masses of people and honking taxis, police cars, and buses jammed bumper to bumper.

Once safely on the lower levels of the Mount of Olives, I wandered around the Garden of Gethsemane and felt a kinship with Jesus. The old olive trees and other plantings imparted a serenity to the place. I could imagine that Jesus found it a peaceful spot to relax or teach His disciples. We read in the Gospels that Jesus periodically had to get out of town, away from the crowds, to rest and pray and have time with His closest friends. I, too, frequently feel that need and desire.

However, this was also where Jesus went to pray after eating His last supper with His friends. It's the place where He was betrayed by one of His own disciples and arrested. Those remembrances brought a somber feeling.

Next to the Garden of Gethsemane is the Church of All Nations, built over the rock where Jesus is thought to have prayed as His disciples fell asleep and the hour of betrayal approached.

The Old City

A steep and winding road leads upward toward the summit of the Mount of Olives. It's also a narrow road; occasionally, it was necessary to stand back and press myself against a wall so that traffic could pass by.

Halfway up the slope is a small chapel, designed to resemble the shape of a teardrop. Built in 1954, it's called *Dominus Flevit*, which means *The Lord has wept*. From there and also at the top of the Mount, we had a beautiful view of the city of Jerusalem. Jesus would have had that view, too, as He came over the Mount of Olives and approached Jerusalem. He gazed across the Kidron Valley and wept over the city's refusal to accept Him. In the landscape He surveyed, of course, the buses, taxis, blocked Golden Gate, and the Dome of the Rock would have been absent.

Another church on the Mount of Olives was built at the place where tradition says Jesus taught His disciples how to pray—giving us what we call The Lord's Prayer. Yet another church at the pinnacle of the Mount is the Russian Church of the Ascension. I was reminded often of Craig's perspective on many of these sites: "If not here, then near."

Today the Mount of Olives is not covered solely with graveyards and churches. There's also a hotel, colleges, and businesses. But I can imagine Jesus standing on the Mount today, looking out over the city, still with tears in His eyes.

. . .

We returned to the Old City through the Lions' Gate, so called because of two lions carved into the walls on either side of the gate, and followed a road called *The Via Dolorosa*, meaning *The Way of Sorrow*. This narrow street winds its way to The Church of the Holy

Sepulchre. Many pilgrims follow the Via Dolorosa, reflecting on the suffering of Jesus as He carried His cross to Golgotha. Fourteen stops along the way, called *Stations of the Cross*, commemorate incidents that occurred as Jesus went from His appearance before Pilate to being laid in the tomb. For example, one station marks the place that Jesus fell the first time; another, the point at which Simon of Cyrene helped Jesus. Again, there are commemorative chapels and shrines built along the way or near to these places.

The Via Dolorosa is probably not the route Jesus actually walked to Golgotha. Historians and archaeologists have been unable to determine exactly where Jesus would have been tried before Pilot; thus, since the very first Station of the Cross marks the point at which Jesus was condemned to death, this puts the entire route in question. Instead of being an exact re-enactment of Jesus' steps, it has become more of a religious pilgrimage that people walk to remember what Jesus suffered for each of us.

The Via Dolorosa starts in the Muslim quarter; its length is about two thousand feet. However, without an experienced guide, a pilgrim could have a considerably longer walk. The maze of narrow side streets requires a sharp eye for the signs that designate the route. Shops and vendors line both sides of this road. Besides being a somber walk of remembrance, it's a marketplace, where trinkets, souvenirs, and mementos of one's trip can be purchased. The finest artifacts depicting the life of Christ and Jewish life in general have been shipped in from lands afar. From China, these artifacts have arrived by the boatload. The Via Dolorosa can be lost in the busyness of commerce.

The trinkets and religious souvenirs held little interest for me. I was, though, enamored with the fruit stands. Mounds of oranges, grapefruits, and pomegranates awaited their destiny in the hand-operated fruit presses. I'd first tasted pomegranate juice back in Capernaum, and now I happily handed over five American dollars to savor the delightful taste again. The juice refreshed me as I sat and watched the masses passing by. Folks of all nationalities were either shopping or walking along, reflecting on the events that happened in these streets.

Reinvigorated, we again set off in search of the church built at the place where Jesus was supposedly crucified and buried. I'm sure you've noticed my frequent use of the word *supposedly* or a synonym. What I can say unequivocally, though, is that being in Israel was bringing the Bible to life for me. I may not have seen the *exact* spot where Jesus prayed in Gethsemane or even where He was buried, but I was seeing and understanding many things about His life that I'd never comprehended before.

Arriving at the Church of the Holy Sepulchre, we were met with a massive crowd. I was simultaneously overwhelmed and underwhelmed.

I was overwhelmed by the number of people who were gathered in the complex of buildings constructed on sites where tradition says Jesus was crucified and buried. I was amazed at the emotions expressed by many of those who had made the pilgrimage to come to this place. Some were on bended knees, weeping.

But I felt nothing—except confusion that I felt nothing. Shouldn't I also be overcome with emotion? This was a place to contemplate the events that are the foundation of all that I believe. A silver disc marks the spot where tradition says the cross was placed, and burial caves are still visible in one section of the church complex.

But the maze of shrines and chapels and distinct areas controlled by six different churches did not feel like a hallowed destination in my own pilgrimage. I had been touched more profoundly on the shore of Galilee, when I talked with Jesus about being a disciple.

Was it the crowd, with many jostling for positions? Was it the idea in my head that kept saying, *But Jesus was buried outside the city walls?*

As I reflect now, I think the reason for my lack of response to that place was because I know Jesus is not dead. He may have been buried there, but He was resurrected and is very much alive. Remember the words of the angel? "He is not here, but He is risen, just as He said."

This place was not the ending. It was only the beginning.

However, I did find it encouraging that so many folks are interested in the life and death of Jesus, and, as I have written elsewhere, we pilgrims may look different and worship differently, but we all have one home in mind.

. . .

Although there is enough to see and do in Jerusalem to fill many days of sightseeing, there are also countless opportunities to explore the surrounding regions. Every day, tourists have dozens of options for day trips outside the city. For folks who aren't traveling with a specific tour, the Abraham Hostel is a great resource. There, you can book tours into the surrounding areas, make arrangements for transportation, or simply get directions and information. Craig and I frequented that place numerous times while we were in Jerusalem.

Lee and Mike were staying at the Abraham Hostel; and when we met them for supper on Wednesday evening and compared notes on our experiences in Israel, I mentioned that there were several locations I still wished to visit.

It turned out that the Abraham Hostel was offering a tour that would encompass three of those places, and so the four of us agreed to meet early the next morning for the tour—leaving the hostel at 3:00 a.m.

CHAPTER 20

Sunrise and Salt

At 2:30 the next morning, Craig and I were walking back to the Abraham Hostel. We were headed into the Judean desert to witness the rising of the sun.

A short distance outside Jerusalem, our driver stopped at a checkpoint. We were entering the area known as the West Bank, and Israel has these checkpoints set up in numerous locations around the West Bank perimeters. Certain areas in the West Bank are very dangerous for Jews to enter, and posted signs warn them to keep out. It's even illegal for Jewish citizens to enter those areas.

Our bus driver was Jewish, and even at that early hour, he was happy to inform us about everything political concerning the West Bank and the dispute between Israel and Palestine over its control. The following day, I traveled to Bethlehem, also in the West Bank, with a Palestinian guide and listened to *his* instruction. As you can imagine, the two didn't quite agree.

Like so many situations in Israel, the "facts" are a matter of perspective. Even "historical" accounts are tinged by bias.

Nevertheless, I shall take a stab at it, and make it as simple as I can—which I realize is ridiculous, since it is anything but simple. Yet I soldier on.

The West Bank is an area encompassing about 2,200 square miles lying to the west of the Jordan River. The Jordan River defines the border between Israel and Jordan. If one was to simply look at a map, the land of the West Bank would seem to be a part of Israel. It juts right into the midsection of Israel. Certainly, many Israelis consider it part of Israel and even call it *Judea* and *Samaria*. A few of the major towns in the West Bank are Hebron, Nablus, Jericho, and part of Jerusalem.

In 1948, Jordan captured this territory during the Arab-Israeli war. In 1952, Jordan annexed it and claimed it as their own, giving Jordanian citizenship to all the inhabitants of the West Bank. However, only a few countries recognized this as legitimate. After the Six-Day War in 1967, the West Bank was put under Israel's control.

Twenty years later, what became known as the First Intifada (meaning *uprising* or *rebellion*) began as Palestinians in the West Bank began to rebel against the Israeli control. Shortly after, in 1988, King Hussein of Jordan had enough of sending money and resources to the West Bank and severed ties with the area.

Fighting continued, until a Declaration of Principles was signed on September 13, 1993, between Israeli Prime Minister Yitzhak Rabin and the Palestine Liberation Organization negotiator, Mahmoud Abbas. This agreement became known as the Oslo Accords and established rules and principles for self-government of the Palestinian people. It would have turned over control of most of the West Bank to the Palestinians. On their part, the PLO agreed to recognize Israel as an existent state and renounce terrorism and its stated desire to annihilate Israel.

But even Palestinians are divided. A number of factions contend for the hearts of the Palestinian people, each with differing opinions on the best strategies for securing a homeland for their people. Fatah is an offshoot of the PLO and is the more rational movement. However, in 2006, Palestinian legislative elections were held, and the organization of Hamas won a plurality in the Palestinian Authority. Hamas is the more extreme faction, carrying out suicide bombings and other terrorist attacks. Whereas Fatah is more open to negotiating peace with live Israelis, Hamas prefers to deal with dead ones.

Later in December of 2006, the Prime Minister of the Palestinian National Authority made the following statement: "We will never recognize the usurper Zionist government and will continue our jihad-like movement until the liberation of Jerusalem." That certainly doesn't sound like a good foundation whereupon to build a lasting peace.

If Palestinian leaders dropped their insistence on the destruction of Israel and dropped their weapons, there would be peace. If Israel dropped their weapons, all Jews would be in danger of imminent death. It doesn't take too much intelligence to see who actually prefers to live in peace.

I'm a twenty-five-year veteran of the food service business, and so I can better explain the Palestinian-Israeli dilemma with a food illustration.

Imagine a pie cut in six pieces. The Palestinian people were offered five of those pieces, and Israel kept one. That would seem fair enough, since Israel suffered a sneak attack by neighboring Arab countries in 1967.

Had all those Arab nations succeeded in conquering Israel, how much land do you suppose they would have given back? Possibly a square inch here or there? Not likely. Israel, on the other hand, gave back most of the land they conquered in 1967, hoping for peace in return.

Palestinian leadership ignored what would have been best for their people and scoffed at the five pieces of pie offered. They wanted the whole pie.

Israel is now doing what any reasonable dessert eater would do with declined pie—they are eating away at those other five pieces as they build Jewish settlements on West Bank soil.

The Jewish driver taking us to Masada found it incomprehensible that Palestinian leadership has failed their own people. Even now, they could agree to the terms of many attempted agreements and still have them honored, but they prefer to fight until they take everything and Israel no longer exists.

I am certainly aware that some of my readers will disagree vehemently with my bent toward the Israeli view of events and future prophesy. Even a segment of liberal Israelis disapprove of Israel's expansion into Palestinian lands. I would recommend that you do your own research and reach your own conclusions before either accepting or rejecting my take on the Middle East Mess.

There will certainly be talks about peace and peace treaties for the foreseeable future. If you want to know why the situation came to be and how it will end, the Bible is a good place to start your research.

I'm also available with a menu for other trouble spots in the world. Who knew a career in food service would prepare me to be an ambassador for peace?

. . .

I love to watch sunrises and sunsets, and one of the world's most famous sunrise-viewing spots is on an ancient mountain plateau called *Masada*.

Masada was a fortress built before the birth of Jesus. King Herod had left Jerusalem, fearing an uprising, and he built a palace and settled on the plateau. Only narrow, steep trails accessed the top of the cliffs, a feature that made it a natural fortification.

But in 66 A.D., an extremist Jewish group known as the Zealots attacked and overcame the Roman soldiers who by then were using the site as a military outpost. The Romans were killed and the Zealots claimed the mountaintop plateau for themselves. They had storehouses for food and cisterns that would refill with rainwater; and for almost ten years, these rebel Jews held out against any attempt to remove them.

The Roman army built a wall around the base of the cliffs to capture any persons attempting escape, but they weren't making any progress in subduing the Zealots and taking back control of Masada. Finally, they built a ramp to the top of the plateau and constructed a siege tower with a battering ram to crash through the walls. From the top of the walls, the Jews threw rocks down on the road builders to hinder their progress. In turn, the Romans used a devious tactic: They forced Jewish prisoners from neighboring towns to work at the construction, counting on the Zealots' reluctance to kill their fellow Jews.

When the fortress walls were finally breached, the Romans discovered that the besieged group had burned nearly everything and then killed themselves. It is said that only two women and five children were found alive; 960 men, women, and children were dead.

This historic site is now a famous tourist attraction. Thousands come there, not only to remember Masada, but to watch the sun rise over the mountains of Moab to the east.

Getting to the plateau is now easier than in King Herod's day. Tourists of this century can take a cable car to the top of Masada. However, the cable operator was not as enamored with sunrises as we were, and the car did not start running until after the sun had already started its morning journey over the eastern mountains.

Several trails do lead to the top of the mountain. We took one called the *Snake Trail*—probably due to all the switchbacks on the hour-long trek to the top. It was an eerie walk, up the dark cliff, with only flashlights to guide our steps. With us were Lee and Mike and about ten other people who had also been on our tour bus; every now and then I could hear quiet mumbling between several people, but the darkness hid us from each other and made us feel isolated.

We reached the top just as light was beginning to touch the sky. The panoramic view from Masada was spectacular. I pondered the events that had taken place there. Had the Jewish holdouts ever taken time to enjoy the beauty that awaited them every morning as the sun peeked up over those distant mountains?

As I pondered the past, brilliant rays shot upward from behind the mountains of Moab. The sun, still unseen, began to fill the surrounding Judean desert with its light. The world slowly warmed as the golden sun appeared and cast its powerful beams on the Dead Sea below, where the Jordan River ends its journey.

· · ·

The tour had also scheduled a stop at the Ein Gedi Nature Reserve. This is an oasis in the desert, one of the prettiest spots in Israel. It's a lush area with waterfalls, beautiful gardens, and hiking trails and is home to much wildlife, including Israel's largest herd of ibexes. The ibex has impressively long, curved horns and is a type of mountain goat, although its body looks more like the deer we see in my home area.

David hid out in Ein Gedi when Saul was pursuing him, and it's easy to see why he chose this area. The craggy cliffs have many caves and rocky lookout points. The waterfalls are fed by four springs, providing a plentiful supply of fresh water.

Our tour group took time to relax at a pool at the base of a waterfall that tumbled down the side of a cliff. Some waded into the knee-deep water and even stood under the falling stream, and I wondered if David's ragtag bunch of men had also been refreshed at this very spot.

. . .

Back in the summer of 1969, two friends and I set off to discover America. We left home with a few dollars in our pockets, a vehicle, and a tent. Meandering the highways and byways of our country, we visited national parks and places we'd heard and read about but had never seen. For us that summer, "places of interest" could be just about anything, anywhere.

One day in Utah, we happened upon the Great Salt Lake. What I'd heard about this lake sounded too good to be true—it was said that a person with no swimming ability could stay afloat in these waters. Of course, we had to test that for ourselves.

The three of us did indeed spend several hours proving the facts about that saline solution. We felt and looked very much like fishing bobbers as we floated along in the brine. We were also being preserved much like salted fish, but we rolled along merrily in the deep blue sea, unsuspecting, and all seemed well.

The 13ᵗʰ Disciple

Upon exiting the lake, we discovered that we were coated with a fine layer of white salt. But "coating" implies that the salt residue could be brushed or blown off. Perhaps I should use the word "encased." That might be more accurate. Although floating in saltwater is supposedly a good treatment if you have a skin condition, we had over-stayed the five-minute duration of a beneficial soak by about two hours. And we didn't have a skin condition—at least, not until we exited the waters.

The day was drawing to a close and we still needed to find a place to pitch our tent. We three salt blocks drove away, seeking shelter. And then the salt began to itch.

Sometime between finding a tent site and finally cleansing myself in the shower, I'd made an irrevocable promise: I would never again in this lifetime enter another salty sea, ocean, pond, pool, or bathtub.

. . .

After leaving the lushness of the nature reserve at Ein Gedi, we were headed to the Dead Sea. This sea is also known as the Salt Sea, and for good reason. It is twice as salty as the Great Salt Lake. It's also ten times saltier than the world's oceans.

In Bible times, Sodom and Gomorrah were two towns bordering this sea. Today, Jordan is on the eastern shore; the southern half of the western shore is Israeli territory; and the northern half of the western shore is considered the West Bank. That part of the West Bank would be Palestinian land; however, Israel controls it since, well, it's part of that pie Israel is nibbling at because the Palestinian leaders aren't yet hungry enough to want a piece of the peace pie.

The Dead Sea is the lowest point on earth. That fact, in itself, was a reason for me to visit. Since it's highly unlikely I will ever visit the highest spot on earth, at least I can say I've seen the lowest.

The Dead Sea used to be about fifty miles long and eleven miles across at its widest point. Those were the dimensions once upon a time. The country of Jordan has diverted large amounts of fresh water from the Jordan River before it empties into the Dead Sea, so the body of water is actually shrinking.

Water enters this lake but does not exit; from the 394-square-mile surface, seven million tons of water evaporate every day. This leaves rich deposits of minerals in the mud. Billions of dollars' worth of minerals such as potash, salt, magnesium, and calcium chloride are removed from the Dead Sea every year.

Many of these minerals are touted as having great health and beauty benefits. At the Dead Sea, wallowing in the mud is considered a healthy thing. The mud can also be purchased for home use, if you don't wish to enter the salty mess.

Of course, one can also float in this sea. Many do. Actually, most visitors do. Everyone in our group except one floated in the saltwater and wallowed in the mud. I imagine you know who remained on dry ground.

The memory from nearly fifty years ago still lingered, so while the rest of the group bobbed and wallowed, I reclined in the shade, enjoying another refreshing glass of freshly squeezed pomegranate juice.

Oh, yes, I did purchase four containers of mud to bring back home—for medicinal purposes only, not beauty treatments.

. . .

When our tour returned to Jerusalem, Craig and I stopped in at the Abraham Hostel again to make arrangements for a ride to "Oh

Little Town of Bethlehem" the next morning.

I remembered that when Jesus and I had that conversation on the beach back by the Sea of Galilee, I had suggested we meet for supper in Jerusalem. I'd be going to the supper the next day, but in order for the meeting to come off as planned, Jesus would first have to be born.

(Yes, I know I'm scrambling the chronology of Jesus' life, but humor me.)

Have you ever gone on a vacation that you've dreamed about for a long time? You may have anticipated a visit to a natural wonder or a man-made spectacle or a highly praised destination. You undoubtedly had conjured up images of what it would be like—only to realize, upon arrival, that your imagined trip was more pleasing than the actual visit.

If you have been thus disillusioned and do not wish another such disappointment, you may want to skip the next chapter, cling to your image of the little town of Bethlehem, and remain in Jerusalem until Craig and I return.

CHAPTER 21

Bethlehem

Back in 1865, when Phillips Brooks, an Episcopal priest from Philadelphia, visited Bethlehem, it was still a "little town." Like so many of us before and after him, Mr. Brooks was visiting the sites of significance in the life of Jesus and one night rode out on horseback to the fields where, possibly there or somewhere near, the angels proclaimed good tidings to shepherds watching their sheep. From his thoughts as he observed those night scenes, Brooks wrote a hymn for the children of his Sunday School.

You might guess that "Oh Little Town of Bethlehem" is among the most popular Christmas songs. As we are headed to the Christmas village, allow me to bring you up to speed on the most popular Christmas songs ever written and recorded. (Please, allow me. I need to do this—it's so much easier than trying to explain the confusing and tangled web of Israeli-Palestinian relationships, and my brain needs the break today.)

Sadly, in the listing I found, "O Little Town" did not even place in the Top Ten. I found it interesting, though, that the top six were all sacred songs. Number 7 was the first secular Christmas lyric—"White Christmas." Numbers 9 and 10 were the other two secular songs in our countdown. "Jingle Bells" took ninth place and the Number 10 slot went to "The Christmas Song." (I can almost see you shake your head and hear you mumble that you've never heard of that one. I hadn't, either, until I realized that we recognize it as "Chestnuts Roasting O'er an Open Fire.")

The Number 1 Christmas song is probably not a surprise to anyone. "Silent Night" outpaced "Joy to the world" by a factor of two. The remaining five were Number 3, "O Holy Night"; Number 4, "What Child is This"; Number 5, "Away in a Manger"; Number 6, "O Come all ye Faithful"; and Number 8, "Ave Maria."

That's all bonus material for you, my friend. Possibly one of those songs is already stuck in your mind. A few Christmas melodies should certainly put us all in the Christmas spirit any time of the year.

. . .

While we drive toward Bethlehem, we'll have a history lesson.

You don't like history, you say?

Keep humming those Christmas carols, and pay attention. History can be very informative. In this case, the details will also fracture your image of the quaint Christmas manger scene. I'll be gentle, though. I promise.

Bethlehem has played important roles in Israel's history, from early Biblical times right up to the modern-day conflicts between Muslims, Jews, and Christians.

Most of us recognize it first as the birthplace of Jesus. It was also the birthplace and childhood home of Jesus' ancestor, King David.

In the fields outside of the town, David, the youngest son of Jesse, was given the job of watching his father's sheep. I can imagine him out there, constantly surrounded and moved by the glories of God's creation. He wrote psalms and praises to God, and in so doing, became "a man after God's own heart." We tend to forget that it was God Himself who coined that phrase to describe David. Wouldn't that be something to be described by God in that way!

Israel had a king, but he had disobeyed God, and God declared that the kingdom would be taken away from him and given to someone else. The prophet Samuel was sent to Bethlehem to anoint the man God had chosen as future king—a young man who no one had even thought to bring in from the fields to meet the messenger from God.

And how did David happen to be born in Bethlehem? You've probably read the story numerous times but possibly didn't connect all the dots. I'll be your dot connector today. All of you pastors, priests, rabbis, and students of God's Word already know this answer, so you can skip this history class if you so desire.

A famine hit Judah, and Elimelech, a man from Bethlehem, and his wife, Naomi, moved out of the country, seeking a more prosperous economy. They had two sons, Mahlon and Chilion. (Not many children are given the Biblical name of "Chilion" in today's society.)

The family crossed the Jordan River and settled in Moab. Remember the sun coming up over the Moab Mountains during my excursion to Masada yesterday? Somewhere over in that area is where Elimelech's family began a new life. Unfortunately, Elimelech died. The two sons found spouses, Ruth and Orpah. But soon the sons also died.

Three widows, without any means of support, considered their options. Naomi encouraged Ruth and Orpah to think about remarriage. She, Naomi, would go back to Bethlehem where she had family and the famine had ended. Orpah remained in her homeland, but Ruth insisted on going with her mother-in-law.

Back in Bethlehem, Boaz, a relative of Naomi's, befriended them and ended up marrying Ruth. From that union came a son, Obed, and Obed was the grandfather of David.

Fourteen generations went by, from the time of David until the Israelites were exiled to Babylon. Another fourteen generations passed, and then Jesus entered the family tree.

Just before Jesus was born, the Roman emperor declared that a census must be taken of the entire Roman world and everyone had to register in the town of their birth. That meant Joseph, from the line of David, was required to go to Bethlehem.

That is how yet one more prophecy about the promised Messiah was fulfilled. And how it also happened that Mary and Joseph were in Bethlehem for Christmas.

. . .

Welcome back, all men and women of the cloth who skipped that little history class.

One of my favorite Old Testament stories also focuses on Bethlehem. You'll find this one in 1 Chronicles 11:16-19. It happened during the time when David was king in Jerusalem and he remembered the refreshing water from the well in his hometown. I imagine that as a boy he filled his flask or sheepskin water jug every morning as he left to watch his flocks.

However, the Philistines controlled Bethlehem at the time, so a drink from the well could only be wished for. But three of David's mighty warriors overheard the king's longing remark and fought their way through to the well to bring back water for their king.

David was so humbled by their bravery that instead of drinking the water, he poured it out as an offering to the Lord.

In the years before Jesus' birth, King Herod, the ruler of Jerusalem, built a hilltop fortress near Bethlehem. He wanted it high enough that he could see back to Jerusalem. My guess is that he also wanted people to marvel at his hilltop mansion. Herod had a problem, though: There were no hills high enough to suit him, so he leveled several smaller hills and used that dirt to develop his hilltop site.

Isn't it interesting that this mighty king had his citadel looming over Bethlehem, and quite unknown to him, a real king was about to be born?

Herod had been appointed ruler of Judea by Rome, so when the wise men came and asked about the King of the Jews who had recently been born, Herod went into panic mode. He tried to manipulate the wise men into returning and telling him where the baby was—but they weren't called "wise men" for nothing; they saw right through his lie that he also wanted to worship. When Herod saw that they had ignored his order and they weren't going to be back to give him the information, he ruthlessly ordered the killing of all male children under the age of two. His order came too late; Joseph had already been warned and had taken his family to Egypt.

Our Palestinian guide told us that archaeologists have uncovered bones of small children mixed with adult arms. Moms held on to their boys in terror, and the Roman soldiers chopped off arms to get the child.

The 13th Disciple

. . .

Israel took Bethlehem from Jordan during the Six-Day War in 1967, and then the town returned to Palestinian control in 1995.

Currently, almost thirty thousand people live in Bethlehem. One-third are Palestinian Christians. Jewish citizens are prohibited from entering Bethlehem. Unemployment is in the 25-30 percent range, since Palestinians in Bethlehem can't enter or work in Jerusalem. Jobs that do become available in Bethlehem are typically in the tourist industry.

A twenty-five-foot barrier encroaches on the outskirts of Bethlehem, hemming it in.

In the early 1990s, Israel began to build fences along the borders between Israel's land and the West Bank. They stated that this was a "security barrier," intended to reduce terrorist strikes against Israel. Like everything else, this action was viewed through different lenses. While Israel called it a security barrier, it became known in Arabic as the *wall of apartheid*. Even U.S. news outlets made careful choices of the words they used to refer to the barrier.

Does the wall make for a safer Israel? I imagine that it's difficult climbing a twenty-five-foot barrier with a bomb strapped to your chest. Also, Israeli soldiers shooting at you would make it difficult to carry out your plan.

Are you sometimes frustrated by a temporary road closing? Today along the West Bank borders, families are divided by that wall. Access to jobs and services has been cut off for some folks. Several cities are almost surrounded by the barrier. The disruption to these lives is much more than a temporary road closing.

Bethlehem is one of the cities severely restricted. There's no land for outward expansion. Building sites are at a premium, and buildings are being constructed upward, on top of existing structures, in order to accommodate a growing population.

The barrier runs for 440 miles along the edges of the West Bank. In some places, it cuts into what was designated as Palestinian territory, placing a slice of land that is (or was?) Palestinian on the Israeli side of the barrier, and Israeli settlements have taken root there.

Jesus could no longer walk across the Mount of Olives to go to Mary and Martha's house. A wall now prohibits that route. I'm sure Jesus could figure out a way to get across such a barrier, but Jews and Palestinians can't.

There is certainly irony in the fact that if Mary, Joseph, and Jesus wished to see Bethlehem today, they would be prohibited from entering the town. Also, the shepherds hurrying to town from watching their flocks at night would never get past the checkpoints.

Such is life in the land of strife.

Well, enough about history and walls. Let's go to Bethlehem and see these things that have been made known to us.

. . .

Although we were only traveling about six miles, our trip to Bethlehem would have to be done in two segments. We had booked an Israeli taxi driver to take us to a neutral area; there, we would be met by a Palestinian Christian taxi driver, who would deliver us to Bethlehem. This was all necessary because Bethlehem is in "Area A" of the West Bank, which is under the Palestinian Authority and strictly off-limits for Israeli citizens.

Traffic clogged the roads leaving Jerusalem toward Bethlehem. Just our luck. The Prime Minister of Russia, Dmitry Medvedev, was in town. Apparently, Medvedev's appearance had closed numerous streets, sending additional traffic out on our route.

Outside of Jerusalem, we went through a checkpoint and then our driver pulled over into a turnoff. We got out of the taxi and climbed into another, driven by a Palestinian. There was no interchange between drivers, no sign of tension or hostility. This is just the way life is.

Nearby, a large sign warned Israeli citizens that entering Area A "Is Forbidden, Dangerous to Your Lives and Is Against the Israeli Law."

We were soon within the city, and our Palestinian guide pointed out the approximate borders of the small town of Bethlehem as it would have been in Jesus' day. We had also passed fields where possibly our friends from Luke 2 were abiding. It is true that at numerous places in the Holy Land, different denominations claim different spots as "the place" of an event in Jesus' life. The shepherds' fields are no exception. Several different places claim to be the dark pastures that witnessed angel songs. At one place about two miles outside the city, the Catholic Church has built the Shepherds' Field Chapel. If the chapel is not quite on the exact spot, at least it is near.

A few sheep still grazed in a few fields, but for the most part, fields and shepherds have been replaced by apartment buildings and urban sprawl.

CHAPTER 22

Christmas to Easter

In Bethlehem, Mary and Joseph found the inn, but it was full. No vacancy. Apparently they, too, did not have reservations, and they had to settle for camping out in the stable. So we have developed this quaint image of a little hut-like shelter where the baby king is born. A lamb snuggles in the straw, cattle low, and the baby Jesus awakes—but no crying He makes, says the song. Probably wrong. He was a baby, a human baby. He cried, and did everything else a baby does. Oh—and sorry to burst your final bubble—but there was no little drummer boy pounding on a drum either. Unless that was why the baby Jesus awoke?

In all likelihood, Jesus was born in a grotto, a cave. In ancient times, household structures were often built against a hillside with such a cavern incorporated as part of the building; the cave provided good storage space and protection for animals.

If a cave sounds like a place too cold to put guests and their baby, the accommodations for the night could also have been an enclosure used for holding animals and attached to the main inn. While hiking throughout Israel, I saw this type of structure numerous times.

Even if you can replace the traditional manger scene with these more realistic images, nothing will quite prepare you for Manger Square in Bethlehem.

As we followed a narrow, winding street crowded by buildings on both sides, our guide explained that the route leading to Manger Square had been historically proven to have been the only way into Bethlehem in Jesus' day.

We came out into Manger Square, a large plaza in the city that is now restricted to pedestrian traffic only. Buildings surrounding the square include Bethlehem municipality buildings, a mosque, and the Bethlehem Peace Center. Anchoring the square is the ancient Church of the Nativity, one of the oldest churches in the world.

Before we go inside the church, let's go back in history, way back to the year 327 A.D. A cave in the area was traditionally considered to be the place where Jesus was born. In 327, Constantine the Great commissioned a church to be built over the site. In the sixth century, that church was destroyed by fire and a new one built over the same site. When the Muslims took the city from the Crusaders in the seventh century, they did not destroy the church but built the mosque close by. I thought it was really neat that now in Manger Square, Christians from all over the world are reminded to pray at least five times a day.

Another image that you'll probably need to adjust is just what a "church" looks like. The Church of the Nativity, like the Church of the Holy Sepulchre, is so much more than a single, integrated building. Over the generations, different denominations have added chapels, convents, and bell towers. The compound of the Church of the Nativity includes a chapel dedicated to Joseph and one commemorating the infants killed by Herod. Tombs are also part of the church.

The Church of the Holy Sepulchre in Jerusalem is overseen by six different denominations: the Greek Orthodox, Armenian Apostolic, Roman Catholic, Coptic Orthodox, Syriac Orthodox, and Ethiopian Orthodox churches. Each has their own territory in the vast complex, and boundaries are jealously guarded. The Church of the Nativity is under the authority of four churches: Roman Catholic, Greek Orthodox, Armenian Apostolic, and Syriac Orthodox.

A major renovation project is currently taking place in the Church of the Nativity, and I imagine that reaching consensus on the details took the skills of the best arbitrator in Bethlehem. The divisions and disagreements in many churches in America today seem minor compared to the negotiations necessary in these complicated churches. I was told that arguments do break out between the monks or "holy men" who live or work in the complex, and the police must be called.

Nor has Manger Square been immune to the Israeli-Palestinian conflict. The mosque and the church and the Bethlehem Peace Center have witnessed tanks in the square and people under siege in the church.

We joined the lines of people wending their way through the complex. The cave where Jesus was supposedly born is located directly beneath the front of a large, open area of the church. Men who looked to me like monks (but I had no idea what church they might belong to) were seated in the front area around the entrance to the grotto. The area was festooned with many types of silver and crystal lamps and containers hanging from the ceiling. My assumption was that each item has a symbolic meaning.

On either side of this large area, concrete steps led to the grotto below. One set of steps led into the cave, and the other set was used as the exit.

Our guide must have had some pull with one of the holy men. He spoke to one of the seated men, then motioned us to leave the line and join him as he went down the exit steps.

Yes, we then entered the sheepfold by another way. The back door. Oh, according to Jesus, that would make us wolves and thieves. Maybe I should look for another metaphor.

The cave was hung with colorful fabrics and elaborate lamps. The floor was paved in marble. And the grotto was crammed with people. Most of them were coming our way, since we had entered via the exit.

But there it was in front of us. The birthplace of Jesus.

The recess in the wall looked very much like a fireplace. Perhaps it had been the "manger," where there would have been hay and feed for livestock. It was difficult to see a manger, though—the face of the rock has been covered over with silver and marble. On the base of the indentation is a silver star, marking the spot of Jesus' birth. Hanging over the star were fifteen lamps, six belonging to the Greek Orthodox, five to the Armenians, and four placed by the Latin church.

Those visiting this site often reach down to touch the star in reverence. Some get down on hands and knees to kiss it. Was this a moving experience for me? Well, I can say it was—but the "moving" was less about emotions and more about being carried along by the throng of people.

My advice is to stay with your preconceived notion of Away in a Manger. It's really better that way.

But I hasten to add, lest you think I'm not respectful of the birthplace of Jesus, that I don't think Jesus would be impressed with this shrine to His birth. We humans do have a need to venerate and worship, and over the centuries, this is what has evolved as a result— but I think that Jesus would be out on the street, teaching people and helping the hurting.

I am impressed, though, by how many people do find a visit to this church to be an emotional experience. I do not mean to criticize any person who visits these sites and finds them compelling. These are sacred sites, and each of us will experience them differently. I would soon stand in a place that did evoke my own tears. That's why, if you ever do get to Israel, I would advise you to go there and discover for yourself.

As I've noted before, just knowing that I was near the spot where world-changing events took place was inspiring for me. And I was learning to know the human Jesus, the man I had come in search of. This trip was changing my relationship with Him, even if I wasn't weeping when expected.

. . .

On the first leg of our short drive back to Jerusalem, our Palestinian driver told us how the wall had separated his family. He had a sister he could not visit, and she could not visit family members in Bethlehem.

That is who suffers. The Palestinian National Authority could have made life more convenient for their people, but chose not to do so. I believe most Palestinian people are good people, and I sympathize with their hardships. They do deserve better—but that would require better leadership.

. . .

Perhaps the absence of throngs of tourists and rampant commercialism was one reason our next stop was more significant to me. Perhaps it was because there, alone in a quiet place where Jesus' battered body once lay, I received an answer to the question that I've pondered for so long.

I wanted to visit the Garden Tomb. The Church of the Holy Sepulchre claims to encompass the place of Jesus' crucifixion and burial, but there is another site that many have come to believe is more likely Golgotha and the garden where Jesus' body was laid.

The Church of the Holy Sepulchre is inside the walls of Old Jerusalem; gospel accounts say that Jesus was crucified outside the city walls. But it turns out that at Jesus' time, the location of the church would indeed have been outside Jerusalem's walls. The walls that exist now around the Old City were built fifteen or sixteen centuries after Jesus' lifetime.

The Church of the Holy Sepulchre was constructed way back in 325 A.D., over a site that tradition said was the tomb of Jesus. In the nineteenth century, though, a number of scholars and archaeologists began looking at another place that seemed a more likely site of the crucifixion—a hill just north of the Temple Mount. That hill was called *Skull Hill* and did indeed have the shape of a skull. Burial caves were also found close by, along with a cistern and wine press, which seemed to indicate there might have been a garden there also. One of the most influential people supporting this hill and garden as the correct site was British Major-General Charles Gordon. Thus, this grave site became known as "Gordon's Tomb" or "Gordon's Calvary." It's also known as the "Garden Tomb."

I had heard from others who had visited Israel that the Garden Tomb seemed more realistic and meaningful to them than the Church of the Sepulchre. In reality, we cannot be certain of the exact location of many events of Jesus' lifetime.

I wanted to see the Garden Tomb.

Walking along the walls on the north side of the Old City, we passed Damascus Gate, where crowds of people were coming and going—and shopping. This is a busy marketplace, and vendors filled the street both inside and outside the gate. We walked past long rows of vegetables, fruits, meats, fish, olives, dates, and spices. As the crowd swirled around us, I could feel the urgency in the air. It was Friday. Shabbat would soon begin. Folks were out buying food for that special evening meal or hurrying to finish errands, because once Shabbat begins, everything shuts down.

Not far from the Damascus Gate, we found the Gordon Tomb, located in what is now a beautiful garden with pathways winding among flowering plants and trees. Along the pathway, painted tiles decorated with vines and flowers bore Bible verses: "I am the vine and you are the branches. Whoever remains in me and I in him will bear much fruit, for you can do nothing without me. John 15:5." Another sign was titled "Because He Lives" and reminded us that "Eye hath not seen, nor ear heard, neither have entered into the heart of man, the things which God hath prepared for them that love Him. 1 Cor 2:9."

Looming at the back of the garden was the rock formation that many believe is Golgotha. At its base is the tomb. This site's simplicity is a striking contrast to the elaborate and complex churches I had visited earlier: a small doorway and window cut into the white and orange rock wall; several containers of flowers placed nearby; a humble sign indicating the entrance. This, immediately, felt "real" to me.

As we approached, we passed a spot where a small rivulet ran down over the rocks. A tiled sign there said, "Let anyone who is thirsty come to me and drink. Whoever believes in me, as Scripture has said, rivers of living water will flow from within them. John 7:37-38." About six months before Jesus' death, He had shouted out those words during the closing ceremonies of the Feast of Tabernacles.

The churches we'd visited earlier had been filled with a massive crush of people. This garden spot was almost deserted, and after several folks emerged from the tomb, Craig and I entered and stood there alone.

Craig offered a prayer of thanks for what Jesus had accomplished here—or near here.

Then he left, and I was alone in the tomb.

That was the moment when all my travels and travails over the years came together and focused on one thought—the answer to my question of *What does it mean to follow Jesus?*

It means that we love like Jesus loved. It means that the Spirit of Christ is in us.

It means that we live "in Him." We obey His teachings, as He taught His disciples in John 14:15: "If you love me, you will obey what I command."

But what does He command?

John 15:12 goes a long way in explaining: "My command is this: Love each other as I have loved you."

As I stood in that tomb, the magnitude of such great love struck me and brought me to tears.

. . .

In the tomb that day, I was also struck by the gravity of crucifying Jesus. They say perpetrators return to the scene of their crimes. I had done so that day.

We easily blame the entrenched, religious Jewish leadership for killing Jesus. However, the real culprit in this heinous act resides in our own houses. I encourage you—challenge you, even—to put this book down and go take a look in your nearest mirror. Staring back at you will be a person responsible for the death of Jesus.

Do you have the courage to face that reality?

Yes, you and I are the reason Jesus died. He died to redeem us.

In His humanity, Jesus suffered the pain of rejection, mockery, doubt, and, finally, the physical agony of beatings and death. He did that so that I could enjoy eternal blessings in a place He has gone to prepare for me.

I was standing in an empty tomb that represented the greatest love mankind has ever known.

Doesn't a love like that demand some type of response?

. . .

Inside the tomb, above the doorway, these words are carved into a wooden sign: "HE IS NOT HERE—FOR HE IS RISEN."

No other prophet or religious founder can claim that.

Muhammad, the founder of Islam, was buried in Al-Massid al-Nabawi, or the Mosque of the Prophet in Medina, Saudi Arabia. He is still there. He did not have power greater than death.

Siddhartha Gautama, who became known as Buddha, or The Enlightened One, also died and remained dead. He was cremated, but one of his teeth still rests in the Temple of the Tooth in New Delhi, India.

And on and on throughout the history of the world. Religious leaders, whether authentic or charlatans, have died and remained dead. The current carnival barkers claiming to be prophets of God are in the process of dying. They, too, will remain dead. Authentic spokespeople of God will die and remain in the grave like all the rest.

Until someday.

The day will come when all are resurrected to either hear the words, "I never knew you" or "Well done, my good and faithful servant."

CHAPTER 23

"Come and Dine"

In one day, I had time-traveled to both Jesus' birthplace and His three-day resting place in the tomb. Quite a feat, by any measure. And the day still held promise of more.

Walking back to the Old City, we threaded our way through more streets crowded with vendors and hurrying people. Coming from the quiet Garden Tomb, our senses were bombarded with the smells and the hubbub of the busy market.

The time for the evening meal was approaching, and I knew where I needed to be. I had an appointment.

We asked a knowledgeable street vendor for directions. Still, the narrow streets leading to the Upper Room confused us. Finally we arrived at what we thought was our destination. Only after wandering through a maze of buildings known as the David's Tomb Compound did we discover the correct entrance to the Upper Room.

Surely Jesus didn't have that much trouble finding the room He had reserved for the special dinner.

The 13ᵗʰ Disciple

A sign posted on the wall read, "Room of the Last Supper." Beneath the heading was an explanation: "A hall built in the Middle Ages at the place where, according to Christian tradition, Jesus partook of the Passover eve meal with His disciples, just before the crucifixion." Like so many other signs, the words were repeated three times: in English and what I took to be Hebrew and Aramaic.

The Upper Room completely defied any notion I had of that place. The room was moderate in size, with almost no furnishings or decorative objects. The eye is taken immediately by the vaulted ceiling and the soaring Gothic arches supported by huge marble pillars. At one end of the rectangular room was what appeared to be a stage area, where an artificial olive tree perched at the place where the table might have been.

Like so many other buildings in Jerusalem, this room bears the signs of the ongoing conflict between Christians and Muslims. Built as a Christian church, it was used as a mosque when the Muslim Ottoman Empire controlled all of the city. Stained glass windows have Arabic inscriptions, and there is the usual niche in the wall that indicates the direction of Mecca, the direction in which one must pray.

Off to my left, a Christian group formed a circle, held hands, and began singing "Alleluia." Here we were, standing on—or near—the spot where Jesus ate His last meal with His closest circle. The repeated words, *Alleluia, Alleluia,* reverberated softly, reverently, throughout the building.

The beautiful melody brought a mist to my eyes.

I blinked several times to clear my vision. Was it my imagination? Or was I really seeing the scene? The stage area filled with men around a table. What a group it was! They ranged in looks from handsome to rather ordinary-looking fellows.

One man looked at me and nodded in greeting, as if he knew me.

It was Him—the man from the shore of the Sea of Galilee.

I had mentioned to Him that I would be in Jerusalem and would meet Him for supper. Nevertheless, I was taken aback that He recognized me.

I pointed to myself, then in the direction of the table, with eyebrows raised in question.

Jesus nodded.

"Come," He said, and heads turned to see who He was inviting to the table.

I approached the steps leading up to where the men were seated. Jesus rose and motioned me to a seat in front of the table. A basin had been set there, on the floor beside a stool.

Jesus came around the table to greet me. *Should I shake His hand? Bow?*

"Sit here," He said, before I could decide what to do.

I sat down.

Then He took off His outer robe, laid it aside, and knelt down in front of me. I knew what was coming next.

He untied my tennis shoes and pulled off my socks.

I was very uncomfortable with this. I pulled my bare feet back, away from His hands.

"Isn't a servant supposed to be doing this?" I asked.

Jesus looked up at me and smiled.

"You want to know what it means to follow Me, don't you? I'm showing you."

"But …"

Jesus reached out and pulled the basin closer, then grasped my ankle and put my right foot in the water. Then my left.

231

When He finished and rose, He looked me in the eye and said quietly, "I've given you an example, Paul. Follow it. Do for others what I've done for you."

He picked up His robe and put it back on.

I was still barefoot. I didn't know what to do next. Thank Him? Excuse myself? Would I be invited to eat with these men? I was hoping.

Just squeeze me in somewhere and let me have an hour here with You. You can put me down there by the end of the table, maybe beside Judas.

But no, what happened then went beyond even my sometimes-outlandish imagination. Jesus motioned for His friend John to move over a bit and ushered me to the seat right beside Him.

The other men were looking at me, then at each other, then back at me again. I saw a few of them muttering to their neighbor. One or two were eyeing my tennis shoes and blue jeans, too.

"This is my 13th disciple," Jesus said to the rest at the table. "I met him back in Galilee, and he volunteered, but I'd already picked you twelve, so he's good with the number 13. He comes from the future."

Now I was under intense scrutiny. There was no more whispering, just stares. A traveler from the future? What could this mean?

Someone down at the end of the table did not seem at all pleased with a last-minute guest. In retrospect, I wonder if *that one* might have been Judas.

"We didn't plan on guests," he said. "Will there be enough food?"

"Where is your faith?" Jesus asked. "Have you forgotten the five thousand, or the four thousand over in the far country? There is always room at my table for one more. Everyone who desires the bread of life is welcome to come and dine."

Music was filling the room, a familiar melody drifting around

me. My dad's rich bass voice was leading a chorus singing words I'd
known from childhood:

> Jesus has a table spread
> Where the saints of God are fed,
> He invites His chosen people, "Come and dine";
> With His manna He doth feed
> And supplies our every need:
> O 'tis sweet to sup with Jesus all the time!
>
> "Come and dine," the Master calleth, "Come and dine";
> You may feast at Jesus' table all the time;
> He Who fed the multitude, turned the water into wine,
> To the hungry calleth now, "Come and dine."
>
> (Charles B. Widmeyer, 1906)

At many supper times in our household, my dad would sound
that call. My siblings and I could be outside playing or scattered
about the house when the invitation came: "Come and dine!" And
as a family, we gathered around a table, fellowshipped, and dined.
Now, with the perspective of 20/20 hindsight, I realize what a sacred
time that was.

And now I was dining with Jesus!

I didn't know how long my time there would last, so I had to
get a few words in before I left that scene. I felt as though I had to
warn Jesus. Ridiculous, I admit, since we all know how this evening
was going to end. But could I somehow change things? Was there
another way?

"Jesus," I said in a low voice as the supper went on. "Don't stop
in Gethsemane tonight. Keep walking over the Mount of Olives and

get to your friends' house in Bethany. That man down at the end of the table who is scowling at me is not your friend."

Jesus looked at me, and I was dismayed to realize that I had just said almost the same thing His friend Peter once told Him. Jesus had been very harsh with Peter. *Get away from me, Satan!* He had said. *You're a dangerous trap to me.*

But Jesus was a little easier on me.

"I know all about Judas. But it is Passover. A sacrifice must be made. And from tomorrow forward, the angel of eternal death will have to pass over you when it sees my blood on your doorpost. No," He gave a slight shake of his head, "I love you and others too much not to tarry in Gethsemane tonight."

. . .

The notes to "Alleluia" were increasing in volume, overriding "Come and Dine" and my dad's voice. I was again surrounded by tourists. A quick glance told me the stage was empty, save for that artificial olive tree.

My imaginary supper with Jesus was just that—imaginary. There is, however, a feast available for those who hunger and thirst for Jesus. And another banquet is being readied for whoever wants to come, in a place Jesus is preparing for all His followers.

"Come and dine," He invites.

I've sent in my RSVP.

How about you?

. . .

It was Friday afternoon. The sun was moving steadily toward the horizon, and Shabbat would soon begin. Craig and I decided to spend several hours at the Western Wall, quietly contemplating the approaching Sabbath.

The scene was very different from my first visit to the Wall. Hundreds of people hurried this way and that through the concourse, intent on doing their prayers and readings before they must be off the streets and home. In the plaza were stacks of white plastic chairs—help yourself, take one wherever you needed to sit. Many were already in rows or drawn in circles around the area. Craig and I each grabbed one, and we settled in to observe this important time in Jewish life.

I noticed that as people entered, the women turned to the right of a low fence, the men to the left. Separate sections for men and women has been the custom since Israel took back control of the Wall in 1967. However, beginning already in the '80s, activists have been pushing for women to be given the right to lead prayers and read from the Torah scrolls at the Wall—a privilege they did not previously have. Orthodox Jewish rules say that women cannot carry or read from the Torah, or even wear religious accoutrements (like the phylacteries or prayer shawls) at the Wall. The battle is between Jew and Jew, the ultra-Orthodox against the liberal. At this site, considered "the place where the Divine presence always rests," people have shouted and argued, one side pushing for their "rights," the other side demanding adherence to the "rules." Women have even been arrested for wearing a prayer shawl or smuggling in a Torah, actions that defy the regulations of the religious authority that oversees the Western Wall Plaza.

At the entry, a sign asks people to be "appropriately and modestly dressed so as not to cause harm to this holy place or to the feelings of the worshipers." There was quite a variety of dress. Most of the men were in black suits and white shirts. Some coats were calf length.

Several men were dressed completely in white, from their white hats to their white shoes, with white cloaks around their shoulders. I had no idea what role they played, but they walked with purpose.

There were many Orthodox Jews with the long side curls.

Head coverings seemed to vary. Some men wore a yarmulke; others had a black hat that looked very much like the dress hats worn by my Amish neighbors. I saw one huge black hat that looked more like a hat box. The women, too, covered their hair.

Quite noticeable were the soldiers in brown, carrying weapons. They, too, wore yarmulkes.

Add to the milling crowd a good mix of tourists from many lands and in many types of garb, and you'll have a sense of the crowd in the plaza that evening.

Small groups gathered, each clustering around a man who seemed to be the leader, reading from what I assumed was the Torah. The books were brought out from a building off to the side of the plaza. The white plastic chairs were in use everywhere, and lecterns were available. It looked like Bible classes, to my Mennonite mind. Often an older gentleman was reading to younger boys. I did notice one ceremony that looked like a bar mitzvah, with a young boy surrounded by family.

People came and went. They read in groups and prayed at the Wall. Groups sang. Most seemed to be in a hurry. Tourists wandered about. At first glance, the scene looked chaotic, but I could sense that for Jews, this was the place they needed to be in the hours before their holy day began.

Out in the center of the concourse sat a yellow cat. He'd somehow slipped through security, but prayers at the Wall didn't seem to be on his agenda. He sat quietly, watching the crowd. We didn't pay much attention to him until he padded over to us and took up a position right underneath my chair.

Behind us, an old fellow napped in a white plastic chair. It was difficult to imagine who or what he was. He had a short white beard; wore a black T-shirt, suspenders, and blue pants; and topped off his outfit with a white fedora with a black band. His feet were bare, his tennis shoes lay at one side, next to a bag of some sort. He didn't seem to be a tourist or a native. And he certainly didn't seem to be someone who would have any interest in the spirituality or symbolic significance of this place. His chair was backed up to a wall. He just looked like a weary traveler passing through, taking a quick nap.

I noticed him immediately because he seemed so out of place in this scene. The image he created, slumped in his chair, chin on his chest, bare feet and suspenders, appealed to my imagination.

The cat had been under my chair for some time when the man behind us woke, stretched, and put on his shoes. Picking up his bag, he rose and began walking our way.

As he passed my chair, he looked at me and gave a small nod toward the cat.

"Lion of Judah," he said, and went on his way.

While we sat and observed life in the hours before Shabbat, we were fortunate enough to witness a ceremony that the Israeli soldiers conduct on Friday evenings. They formed a large circle on the concourse, arms around each other's shoulders, and chanted, sang, and danced.

The day was waning, and above the Western Wall we could already see the pale orb of the almost-full moon. It was one day before the supermoon of November 2016. The next day, Shabbat, the full moon would be the closest to earth it has been since 1948, the year Israel fought their War of Independence and the State of Israel was born.

Over all of this activity and commotion, the Muslim call to prayer blared out over the plaza. I pondered whether Muslims in Mecca would tolerate a Christian call to prayer in that city most holy to them. I didn't ponder long. I knew such a thing wouldn't be tolerated.

It might be a good thing for American Christian churches to erect speaker systems in their own spires and sound calls to prayer several times a day. It seems many of our churches are too timid and fear they might offend someone.

Muslims are not timid about what they believe.

But why five calls to prayer a day?

I'm glad you asked. You might find the story hard to believe. Matter of fact, I don't believe it myself. It illustrates, though, how much faith factors into our religious beliefs.

We Christians believe many things that folks outside of Christianity can't accept. We believe God created the world. We believe in a virgin birth. We believe our king died but was resurrected and lives today. As a Christian, I may not understand how God achieved all this, but my faith compels me to believe.

Here's the background story concerning the five calls to prayer, a story that's known as the Night Journey.

The angel Gabriel brought a steed to Muhammad. Well, at least, it was a beast of some kind that was used to transport the prophets. Called *Buraq,* this animal was pictured as having a human face and a horse's body, equipped with wings. White, and smaller than a mule but larger than a donkey, Buraq had a stride that reached as far as it could see. On Buraq, Gabriel and Muhammad traveled from Mecca to Jerusalem, to the point where the mosque stands on the Temple Mount. Thus, this spot became a sacred site for Muslims.

On Mt. Moriah, Muhammad prayed before the Night Journey

continued. Then on into the heavens they went—through a series of heavens, actually, meeting people we know as Biblical figures and prophets. Finally, Muhammad met and conversed with God, who instructed Muhammad to have his followers pray fifty times a day. That certainly doesn't leave much time to get into any major projects, and it almost matches the exhortation we Christians have received to pray without ceasing.

Muhammad also talked with Moses, who must have thought God misspoke because he encouraged Muhammad to go back to God and implore Him to reduce that requirement. God obliged and agreed to ten times, then finally assented to only five daily prayers.

Back to Mecca went Buraq to return Muhammad to his followers, who then received this command of God and follow it to this day.

And that is why, as I sat at the Western Wall, I heard the Muslim call to prayer while the Jews prayed their prayers and read from their Torah.

Yes, I find the story hard to believe. However, now that I think about it, we Christians believe a story that probably sounds just as outlandish. It's told in Numbers 22 and is about a talking donkey.

. . .

Craig and I headed back to our room. The sun had set, and Shabbat had begun. Everything shuts down for the Sabbath. The rail system does not run. No taxi can be found. Stores close. For Jews strictly observing the Sabbath, it is forbidden to work, to ride in a vehicle, or even to switch electricity on or off. Businesses that cater to tourists of all religions may have elevators that run as usual, but they will also have at least one Shabbat elevator—one that automatically stops at each floor so that guests are not required to push buttons to choose floors.

The 13ᵗʰ Disciple

Above us was the almost-full supermoon, but the streets were eerie, dark, and mostly deserted. The busy city was suddenly a ghost town. A few stragglers were still out—several gentile cats who didn't adhere to Sabbath rules and a handful of gentile tourists like Craig and myself prowled the streets, looking for sustenance.

What does one do when all purveyors of hummus, falafel, and gefilte fish are shuttered? The choices were quite limited that night. Finally, in a corner building, we ascended a flight of steps and were ushered into a Chinese restaurant.

CHAPTER 24

One Man Must Die

The Sabbath quiet continued on Saturday morning. The streets were emptied of vendors. Although most of the tourist attractions were unattended, one could wander about freely, and Craig and I did just that.

We carefully checked the map for directions to Hezekiah's tunnel and the pool of Siloam, then set off to see these sites.

Within minutes, we were lost.

So we did what many men do in such a dilemma. We kept walking—and went from lost to a potential dangerously lost.

We had wandered a good way into Muslim territory and were being given rather odd sideways glances from the men wandering the streets. They obviously weren't celebrating the Sabbath.

Craig stated the obvious: "We are where we shouldn't be."

A quick backtrack brought us into friendlier environments.

Once again, Craig consulted his map, and we realized we were already standing at the entrance to the Pool of Siloam and Hezekiah's Tunnel.

The story of this tunnel goes back hundreds of years before Jesus' birth.

Judah had been paying a yearly tribute to the mighty Assyrian empire, but King Hezekiah of Judah decided to end that extortion. This defiance caused Sennacherib, the Assyrian king, to begin an invasion of the towns of Judah. Hezekiah relented, and agreed to pay one ton of gold and nearly eleven tons of silver, hoping Sennacherib would go home and end the campaign before the army arrived at Jerusalem. To pay the tribute, Hezekiah stripped the Temple of most of its silver and gold.

Sennacherib collected, of course, but he had no intention of calling off his army as they continued to ransack and destroy towns. Hezekiah realized that Jerusalem would soon be under siege, so he came up with an ingenious plan, described in 2 Kings 20:20 and Chronicles 32:30.

Jerusalem's water source was a spring known as the Gihon Spring. The word *Gihon* translates to *gushing*. From the Gihon—outside the city walls—fresh water was delivered to Jerusalem's inhabitants by an aqueduct. However, this aqueduct would be an easy target for attackers who would want to cut off Jerusalem's water supply and who would also need water for themselves.

Hezekiah designed an alternate plan to supply Jerusalem with water. Two crews of men started at opposite ends and constructed a tunnel that channeled the water from one end of Jerusalem to the opposite end. The two crews eventually met in the middle, having completed a tunnel that extended for 1,750 feet. The tunnel has a bit of an "s" shape to it, and it is believed the workers were following a natural crack in the solid rock.

They closed the aqueduct and directed the waters from the spring into the tunnel. At the other end of this man-made channel, the water was collected in the Pool of Siloam, within the walls of the city.

In the tunnel, tourists can now walk through knee-deep water—on days that aren't the Sabbath, that is. At the entrance to the tunnel, Craig and I were stopped by a locked gate.

Nearby, the Pool of Siloam is being excavated. It is thought that this is the second pool built—Hezekiah's pool may be buried somewhere beneath the city.

The Pool of Siloam had great significance to the Jews, not only as a source of potable water but also as a *mikvah,* a bath for ceremonial cleansing. The ancient pilgrim road leading up to the Temple passed this pool, and folks arriving in Jerusalem would perform their rituals of cleansing there, in order to be acceptably "clean" to enter the Temple area.

The large pool was also the place where a special water ceremony began during the Feast of the Tabernacles.

. . .

God had given commands for a number of holy days to be observed throughout the year. Three of these feasts were "pilgrim" festivals; that is, all male citizens were to travel to Jerusalem for the event, regardless of where they lived. God actually outlined instructions for seven feasts, but to keep things simple here, we'll just look at these three. The feasts were organized around the planting and harvest seasons, but they all have spiritual and historical significance.

The Passover remembered the night that the Israelites were making preparations to leave slavery in Egypt. The blood of a lamb smeared on their doorposts protected the household from the angel of death. This festival coincided with the start of the spring planting season. Jewish calendars were based on the phases of the moon, and thus did not correspond exactly to our modern-day calendar.

A second feast, Pentecost, celebrated the first harvests of late spring. It came forty-nine days after Passover and commemorated the giving of the Torah at Mount Sinai.

The final pilgrimage to Jerusalem was made for the Feast of Tabernacles. When travelers arrived in the city for this eight-day festival, they put up temporary "booths" in which they lived for the week. The festival commemorated the forty years the children of Israel had wandered in the desert, and it was a week marked with great joy at God's past provision and prayers for His continued care. The feast was at the time of the fall harvest, just before the winter rains began.

The Feast of Tabernacles began and ended on a Saturday, each of those days kept as a Sabbath with no work permitted. During the week, sacrifices were made every day and people brought their tithes and offerings. Each day, the trumpets were blown at the Temple, and at night a huge candelabra in the Temple was lit to remind the people of the pillar of fire that led them in the wilderness. The seventh day was called the *great day.* On that day, a spectacular water offering was made to appeal to God to send the winter rains. There was dancing, singing, worship, and praise.

The overall atmosphere of the Feast of Tabernacles was one of joy, as people remembered all God had done for them and prayed for His continued presence with them. The week was a reminder of God "tabernacling" or dwelling among His people. Some look into prophecy and believe that the ultimate fulfillment of God living with His people will come in association with the time of this feast.

That's a very general overview of these three celebrations, and I don't pretend to be a scholar of Jewish history. I am beginning to see more clearly, though, the spiritual significance of these commemorations. The instructions from God were originally given as part of the "Law," the Torah. Jesus came to fulfill the Law, to bring the purposes of the Law to fruition. So we can see that even for Christ followers, these times of remembrance are important.

It is no "coincidence" that Jesus was killed during the Passover week. He was our Passover lamb; His blood delivered us from our slavery to sin and canceled the death sentence against us.

Pentecost, the festival celebrating the giving of the Law at Sinai, is the time when the early church first received the Holy Spirit. Again, not a coincidence. Christians now do not live by the Law, but by the guidance of the Spirit.

And should we not have a celebration akin to the Feast of Tabernacles? You may do this, privately, on an occasion like New Years' Eve, when many people look back and celebrate the year and look forward in hope to the next year. Shouldn't we Christians have some specific time that we celebrate—*with joy!*—how God has provided and led us in the past and then look forward to His continued presence with us as we go into the future? I think so. We may do this individually, but why not a corporate celebration?

If your appetite has been whetted, and you want to explore more fully what these pilgrimages represent and how they can encourage you in your Christian walk, I encourage you to dig into many resources available from scholars more scholarly than I.

We assume that Jesus attended these festivals during His lifetime. Luke wrote that Jesus' parents went to Jerusalem every year for the Feast of the Passover (Luke 2:41). Jesus was a Jew, and He probably made that pilgrimage each year of His life, too.

These holy days took Jesus to Jerusalem, and events there are what God used to finally bring His plan for our salvation to its climax.

That first time we see Jesus going to Jerusalem as the teacher from Galilee was for the Passover. Then, He walked into the Temple, found a marketplace atmosphere, and "cleaned house." He also did miraculous signs during the time He was there for Passover, although we don't know specifically what those were, and many people began to believe in and trust Him. It was on that trip, also, that Nicodemus dared a furtive visit to Jesus to question Him about His teaching. Nicodemus was one of the religious leaders, and it seems He was almost at the point of believing, yet He must have been afraid to be seen talking to Jesus in the light of day.

Jesus spent some time out in the countryside of Judea, teaching His disciples. Then He returned to Galilee, and found that word of His miracles had returned home before He did. Many people had been in Jerusalem for the Passover and had either heard about or saw for themselves the things Jesus did and taught. He was welcomed back in Galilee.

. . .

Sometime later, Jesus made another trip to Jerusalem for another one of the Jewish holy days. While in the city, He walked by another pool—the Pool of Bethesda, that was surrounded by five covered porches. This pool was close to the Lions' Gate, known as the *Sheep Gate* in Jesus' day because that's the gate through which they brought the sheep for sacrifices. It's in the Muslim Quarter.

At this pool Jesus healed a man who had been sick for thirty-eight years.

"Get up," Jesus told the man. "Grab your mat and walk!"

The man was healed instantly and did as told.

Oops.

After thirty-eight years of misery, he experienced a miraculous healing—and immediately ran afoul of the law. It was the Sabbath, and carrying a mat on the Sabbath was forbidden.

The Jewish authorities confronted, accused, and questioned the man. Eventually they got to the root of the problem: That Galilean teacher again!

The Jewish leaders turned to harassing Jesus about breaking the Sabbath rules. Jesus' response didn't help the situation. He said, "My Father is always working, and so am I."

He had called God *His Father*.

That escalated the problem to new heights, and the Jewish authorities began to talk about having this troublemaker killed.

. . .

In the fall of the last year of Jesus' life, the time was approaching for the pilgrimage to Jerusalem for the Feast of Tabernacles. In the Gospel of John, we read a puzzling account.

Jesus had been staying away from Jerusalem. He knew the Jewish leaders were plotting against Him. He had been traveling quite a bit around Galilee, and He possibly made another trip to the far country. Shortly after He visited Caesarea Philippi with His disciples, Jesus had a conversation with His brothers.

As difficult as this is to understand, John's account tells us that Jesus' brothers didn't believe in Him. As they prepared to leave for Jerusalem for the feast, they taunted Him. Why was He doing His work in "secret" in Galilee? *Why hide in Galilee? Get on the big stage in Jerusalem where the crowds are gathering and you can make a name for Yourself!* You can hear the sarcasm, can't you?

Jesus told his doubting brothers to go on ahead because His time had not yet come. What did that mean? Was He looking toward the Passover, which would be the next required pilgrimage about six months later, in the spring?

Even stranger, it seems that Jesus then changed His mind.

The Feast of Tabernacles got underway in Jerusalem. Can you imagine it? Tens of thousands of Jews were gathering there, putting up their temporary shelters, visiting with the folks camping next to them, talking about what had happened in their lives since the last gathering in Jerusalem, anticipating the events of the week, and wondering if they would see "that teacher from Galilee." Folks had expected Him to show up, but no one had seen Him. The rumor was that the authorities were looking for Him, too. Some mentioned quietly that He was a good man. Others decried Him as a deceiver of the common people.

Then, halfway through the week, Jesus appeared in the Temple courts and began to teach.

Those who heard Him were riveted by His words. *Where did He get this knowledge?* they wondered. He hadn't been trained by the leadership in Jerusalem. Jesus' reply was that His teaching came not from Him but from God.

Some who heard Him thought He was demon possessed. Think about that. His message and delivery must have been passionate and penetrating. You couldn't ignore Him or doze off when listening to Jesus! I like the story about the officers sent to arrest Him.

The Pharisees and lead priests were keeping an eye on things, and when they realized how much talk there was about who Jesus was, and about the miracles He'd done, and the whispers, *Could this be the Messiah?* they decided it was time to act. Put a stop to it now, once and for all.

They sent the Temple guards to arrest Jesus.

But the guards were drawn into what was happening in the crowd.

It was the climax of the festival, the last and "greatest" day. Each day of the festival, the ceremony of the Pouring of the Water began at the Pool of Siloam. A priest led a procession down the Pilgrim Path from the Temple. He was followed by a crowd of worshipers. People waved palm fronds, which made a swooshing sound very much like rain gently falling. The ceremony was, after all, a ceremony imploring God to send the winter rains.

The priest filled the pitcher with fresh water from the pool and led the celebrating crowd back though the Water Gate toward the altar in the Temple where the offering would be made. As the priest entered the Temple, He was met by another priest bearing a pitcher of wine from grapes recently crushed.

Flutes, harps, and other instruments were playing. A choir chanted verses from Psalm 118, and a trumpet blast announced the arrival of the water sacrifice. People danced and clapped their hands and stomped their feet. It was indeed a time of joyful celebrating. An ancient rabbi even wrote: "Anyone who has not seen this water ceremony has never seen rejoicing in his life."

The wine and the water were poured out simultaneously at the base of the altar, and the liquid flowed down the Temple steps and into the outer courts.

Then—imagine it—on this last great day, as the rejoicing at the water sacrifice commenced, above the sounds of music and the celebration, a voice rang out. It was that teacher from Galilee, shouting out loud enough for everyone to hear Him.

"If anyone thirsts, let him come to Me and drink. He who believes in Me, as the Scripture has said, out of his heart will flow rivers of living water."

John wrote in his account of this that Jesus was referring to the Holy Spirit, who would be given to everyone who believed in Him after his death and resurrection. But that had not yet happened.

Imagine the crowd's reaction to this strange behavior and even stranger words. The Temple guards listened to the debates going on all around them. What did Jesus mean? And who was He, really? Some said Jesus was a prophet. Others believed He was the Christ. But how could the Messiah come from Galilee? (Apparently, those people hadn't studied the prophecies thoroughly.) Some wanted Jesus arrested; He was demon possessed, or at least, a lunatic; get Him out of here, let's get on with the festival. Others wanted to hear what He had to say.

The guards themselves were fascinated with Jesus' teaching, and they forgot their assignment!

They returned to the priests and Pharisees without a prisoner, shaking their heads, still in awe of the teacher they had heard. "We've never heard anyone speak like that!" they told their bosses.

"You mean, He's deceived you, too?" We can imagine the frustration and fury of the Pharisees.

Then we hear one voice, a bit braver than the last time we met him: Nicodemus speaks up. He was part of that Jewish leadership. He reminded the group about a legal issue: "Our law does not condemn anyone without first hearing from him."

The others turned their fire toward Nicodemus.

"Are you from Galilee, too? Check the Scriptures, buddy. No prophet ever comes from Galilee."

And that comment shows how these folks were losing their heads in their obsession to quiet Jesus. The fact was that Elijah, Jonah, Micah, and a number of other prophets had come from Galilee. They were ignoring the historical and Scriptural record, and even more pointedly, ignoring the prophecy that the Messiah would indeed come from Galilee.

The possibility that this troublemaker was the Messiah? That was something they refused to even think about.

. . .

Of course, we can't be certain that Jesus shouted out those words during the time of the water ceremony, but learning about the feasts and the context in which Jesus spoke many of these words has added greatly to my comprehension of the events in Jesus' life. He lived in a historical and religious setting, in the flow of humanity's history.

Imagine Jesus during that Feast of Tabernacles. He would have been dwelling in some kind of temporary structure set up just for this week. John wrote that Jesus "returned to the Mount of Olives." Did He camp there? Or did He go there to talk with His Father about what was going on? Or does John simply mean that Jesus went there after the festival was over?

But He came back to the Temple again, several times, and continued to talk with all who would gather around Him and listen. Reading the Gospel of John, especially, gives us the sense that Jesus' teaching was gaining intensity and urgency. Later, as He came back to Jerusalem in the spring for another feast (and for His own sacrifice), He would pause on the Mount of Olives, look over Jerusalem, and weep as He said, "How I wish today that you, of all people, would understand the way to peace" (Luke 19:42).

During the Festival of Tabernacles, Jesus used another obvious symbol to point to Himself as the fulfillment of Scripture. The prophetic words are in Isaiah 9:1-2, when Isaiah foretold a great light would come to people walking in darkness. This would occur in Galilee, by the sea and by the Jordan.

One of the traditions of the Feast of Tabernacles was that on the first night, four large candelabras were lit in the Temple. These golden candelabras were nearly seventy-five feet tall, and each had four branches, each branch supporting a large bowl. Four men would climb ladders to fill the bowls with oil—each man's burden was ten gallons of oil. These bowls of oil were then lit, illuminating the entire area. And since Jerusalem was set on a hill and the Temple was on the highest spot in the city, folks near and far could see the amazing display of light.

This represented the pillar of fire with which God led the children of Israel during their time in the wilderness.

It was immediately following the feast that Jesus was teaching in the Temple. It's possible those giant candelabras were still standing. Perhaps Jesus even pointed to them as He spoke the words, "I am the light of the world. Whoever follows me will never walk in darkness, but will have the light that leads to life."

Some choose to accept that as truth. Others choose darkness rather than light.

We all must make the choice.

. . .

During this time in Jerusalem, the Pharisees had tried to arrest Jesus several times, a mob had tried to stone Him, and He had, in general, stirred up quite a commotion. But no harm came to Him because, Scriptures say, it wasn't yet time.

Yes, God has a timetable.

It was during this time, too, that Jesus healed a blind man and then sent him to the Pool of Siloam to wash.

You'll probably remember that the method of healing this time was that Jesus spit on the ground and made a batch of mud which He smeared on the man's eyes. Then He instructed the man to go to the pool and wash. The man did as he was told, and he came back seeing.

Learning about the Pool of Siloam, the ceremonies of washing, and the traditions at the time of Jesus has added much to my reading of the Gospels. Here, Jesus tied the ritual of cleansing—something His blood would do for each of us—to His mission to give sight to the blind. So much of what He did in the physical, earthly context of the world in which He lived can be applied to our spiritual lives today.

I'll say it again—if you have a chance to visit Israel, go!

. . .

Soon after the Feast of Tabernacles was over, Jesus thought it best to go again to the opposite side of the Jordan, where John the Baptist had started his ministry of preaching repentance and baptism. Many people Jesus met there became believers.

He was there when He received word that His dear friend Lazarus back in Bethany had a bad case of about-to-die. Sisters Mary and Martha hoped that Jesus would quickly come and heal their brother. They had faith that He could, so they had sent word: "Hurry."

However, Jesus took His good old time and remained where He was for several more days. When He finally determined to return to Judea, Lazarus was already dead. The disciples weren't too enthused about going back to the Greater Jerusalem area.

"Just a few days ago, they were trying to stone you," they reminded Jesus. A valid objection, the 13th disciple would probably have reasoned.

"But I need to go there to awaken my friend Lazarus," Jesus answered.

"Oh, well, if he's sleeping that's good. He's getting better."

"No, He's dead," said Jesus. "And, for your sakes, I am glad I wasn't there."

And then Jesus added something I find puzzling. He said, "Now you will really believe."

Jesus apparently knew what would happen when they went back to Bethany and found Lazarus already dead and buried. But—is it possible that the disciples were still struggling to have faith in Him? They had seen and heard so much, but were they still not believing He was the Son of God, the Redeemer, the Messiah?

That comment from Jesus seems to say that His chosen circle did indeed suffer from the same malady we do, a shortage of faith when there should be no question of whether or not we can trust Him. And how often we tell God, "Please, hurry and answer my prayer!" But sometimes, He waits—for His glory and for our own good.

By the time Jesus and His disciples arrived in Bethany, Lazarus had been resting in repose for four days. Jesus went to the tomb and requested that the rock closing the burial cave be moved. That suggestion was met with a great deal of reluctance. Understandable. They feared an incredible stench would emanate from within.

"Lazarus, come out," boomed Jesus' voice.

I imagine Jesus had a good timbre to his voice. He shouted at the seas to be still. He shouted during the water libation ceremony at the Feast of Tabernacles. He surely had to speak loudly many times. This time, His words were loud enough to awaken dead Lazarus.

Can you see the people stretching their necks, trying to see if anything's happening? Then, at the mouth of the cave, a specter appears! Not a ghost, but Lazarus, wobbling, since he's still restrained by burial cloths binding him from head to toe.

"Unwrap him!" Jesus commanded.

What a scene that must have been!

This return from the dead brought many to faith in Jesus. We wonder if the disciples were now fully convinced.

In reality, this was not a *resurrection;* it was a *resuscitation.* When Jesus was resurrected, his burial accoutrements were neatly folded up and placed to one side of the tomb. Jesus has a resurrected body; Lazarus did not.

While this event promoted even more belief in Jesus, it put the chief priests and Pharisees into full-fledged panic. Of course they heard about it. News like that travels fast. They had to do something before this teacher from Galilee attracted more followers and they lost all their authority over the people.

The high priest, Caiaphas, now declared that Jesus must die. He made his reasoning sound as though it was for the good of the whole Jewish nation. Of course, he was rationalizing. But he had spoken the great truth of Jesus' mission on earth: One man had to die to save us all.

And so, they began to make concrete plans to do what they had only talked about before—kill Jesus.

Lazarus, who had just been given back his life, was now also marked for death because of the commotion he was causing. Some days, you just can't win.

Jesus stopped appearing in public and went to a wilderness town with His disciples, staying there until the time came for the spring festival, the Passover. Then the sacrifice would be made, the blood of the Lamb would be shed, and the power of the angel of death would be broken forever.

CHAPTER 25

Who Will You Follow?

All these things were on my mind as I sat at the Western Wall again on Saturday night. We had made arrangements for transportation to Tel Aviv early the next morning, and Craig and I had decided to spend our last few hours in Jerusalem at the Wall, watching, pondering, praying.

An extreme aggregation of diverse influences has created the Jerusalem of today. Possibly the most profound manifestation of that is right at the Western Wall, where Jews pray with their faces turned toward the last remnant of their holy Temple, while the Muslim call to prayer carries over the plaza, the golden dome rises above the Wall, and Christians come to contemplate their history and the life of the King they follow.

People of faith. All of us have made a choice of who we will follow. Even those who claim not to believe in any deity still have chosen gods who lead them—whether their gods be other minds and personalities or their own.

The 13ᵗʰ Disciple

In Jerusalem, I found that the traditions and laws of the deeply devout Jews can teach us things that take to new depths our understanding of what Jesus has done for us. We can learn from the Jews ways to better live out our beliefs. We might even increase the joy in our spiritual journeys!

The Jews wait for their Messiah. I wait, too. But my Redeemer has already come to earth, once in a certain time period, and what I wait for is the day He comes back again to bring His kingdom finally, irrevocably, into existence on a new earth.

Side by side with the Jews here in Jerusalem are the Muslims. I recognize that there are devout Muslims who follow The Religion of Peace with good intentions. I have great difficulty, though, understanding how they can follow the leader of that religion.

If Muhammad lived today, his actions would make him a narcissist, a pedophile, a mass murderer, a terrorist, a lecher, a cult leader, a madman, a rapist, a torturer, an assassin, and a looter. His behavior as such is described not only by historians but by his own writings—and he encouraged his followers to follow his example.

These particular descriptive words listed above were taken from the book *Understanding Muhammad* by Ali Sina. The author is a former Muslim, and he did not write to promote Christianity instead of Islam; in fact, he claims to be an atheist. He wrote because he wants people to discover for themselves what that religion stands for. Needless to say, he's not popular with Muslim leaders. They've called for his death.

As Muhammad would have done. Anyone who defied him was killed. Today we see the radical followers of his religion doing the same.

Jesus came into this world to set prisoners free, to heal the sick, and to give sight to the blind. Those actions go beyond the physical—

it is spiritual freedom, healing, and sight that Jesus gives.

In Galatians 5, the Apostle Paul described the attributes of both Muhammad and Jesus quite succinctly. The fruits of a sinful nature, he wrote, are sexual debauchery, idolatry, sorcery, hatred, discord, rage, selfish ambition, and envy. The fruits of Jesus' spirit are love, joy, peace, patience, kindness, goodness, faithfulness, gentleness, and self-control.

In the Old Testament, there is a story about a contest between the God of Elijah and Baal. Elijah told the people to quit vacillating and choose one: "If the Lord is God, follow Him. But if Baal is God, follow him."

The question is rather a simple one: Who do you want to follow?

. . .

The next morning, Sunday, we were in Tel Aviv. My time in Israel was almost at an end.

We had an entire day to spend in the city, so we decided to walk to the port of Jaffa, where Jonah boarded his cruise ship for his underwater adventure.

Since we had plenty of time, we enjoyed a leisurely breakfast at the cafeteria of the Tel Aviv Abraham Hostel. Craig directed my attention to what was happening at another table.

A Hasidic Jewish couple was attempting to eat breakfast. However, we gentiles were also partaking and had apparently defiled the buffet. We had cut off a few slices of bread; the man tore off the end we had touched and then took the remainder of the loaf to his wife. For her part, she objected to the silverware on the table and asked the kitchen for others. Cups and plates were removed and replaced. Then each item of food was scrutinized. Kosher? If not, back to the kitchen the husband went. He was a jack-in-the-box. We were finished with our breakfast before the first bite was lifted to her mouth.

I'm thankful that my King makes it perfectly acceptable to enjoy a good breakfast without all those acrobatics.

Later at the airport, I was again reminded of the freedom I've been given. We were on the plane. Everyone boarded. Ready for takeoff.

But just as we were about to taxi out on the runway, a practicing prayer warrior realized it was time for prayer. While the rest of us looked on in wonderment, he stepped into the aisle, strapped on the phylacteries long and wide, and entered his closet to pray. That is, he flung a prayer shawl over his shoulder and ascended skyward. At least, he ascended in a prayerful manner, leaving all the rest of us stranded on the ground.

No cajoling or badgering from the flight attendants could deter this man from his intended task. Not even the announcement from the pilot, commanding him to take his seat. He would not be convinced to sit down and fasten his seat belt.

So wait on the Lord we did.

I was certainly relieved that Jesus didn't just pass through Gethsemane that night and keep on walking out of town. He paid the price for us so that we don't have to delay a whole plane full of people.

Jesus' one commandment is the perfect fulfillment of the 600-plus rules that are impossible to follow flawlessly: "Love one another as I have loved you."

As dawn was breaking and the land was awaking, our prayer partner unwound his phylacteries and finally took his seat. We then headed skyward, living proof that Isaiah 40:31 is accurate: "They that wait on the Lord ... shall mount up with wings as eagles."

The land of Jesus receded. I caught one last glimpse of the Sea of Galilee. My thoughts turned again to my imaginary meeting with Jesus there on the shore, my desire to be a disciple, and the example He gave me—washing my feet, a chore for servants.

I was to follow His example, He said, and serve.

I'd willingly, gladly wash my children's feet. My neighbors' feet? I'd rather not. My enemy's feet? Serve my enemy? My first reaction was to recoil. *Surely* Jesus couldn't mean that?

Then I remembered something else He had told His disciples: "Praying for and doing good to your enemies makes you a true child of God."

He asks me to follow His example.

He washed Judas's feet. And He knew all along what Judas was going to do that night.

CHAPTER 26

Invitation to the Feast

Judas went through with His plans. He betrayed Jesus and led soldiers to arrest Him. The religious leaders thought they'd won. Satan thought he had won.

That all changed at the tomb.

I can't imagine myself in Jerusalem as the 13th disciple on the day when the women came back from the garden tomb to say that Jesus was no longer dead. I'm not sure if I would have been among the first to rejoice and say, "He did just what He said He'd do!" or if I'd be huddled with Thomas, wondering if the others were hallucinating.

But you can be sure I'd be with the rest of the group when they went back to Galilee because the word was that Jesus had told us to meet Him there. I'd get there as fast as I could. Hitchhike, not walk.

The disciples did return to Galilee and went back to their old way of life—going out fishing. It was a disastrous night, as far as the fishing went. They were returning to shore with not one fish.

On the shore, someone was bending over a fire, and the tired men caught the aroma of fish cooking and fresh bread.

"Friends, how was the fishing?" the person called out.

They gave their mournful tally: not a one.

"You're fishing on the wrong side of the boat. Toss your net out on the other side."

They did, and were amazed when they hauled in a massive amount of fish—more fish than the net should have been capable of holding. They counted the catch and had a total of 153 fish.

Now—can you feel the excitement?—they realized it was Jesus on the shore. Peter jumped into the water and splashed his way to Jesus.

Jesus invited them to breakfast.

The song of "Come and Dine" that I heard at my imaginary supper with Jesus has a second verse:

> The disciples came to land.
> Thus obeying Christ's command,
> For the Master called unto them, "Come and dine";
> There they found their heart's desire,
> Bread and fish upon the fire;
> Thus He satisfies the hungry every time.

At that breakfast, Jesus had yet another mission: reinstating Peter back into good fellowship. Peter had denied Jesus three times at the trial. Now, Jesus asked Peter three times, "Peter, do you love me?"

Each time, Peter replied that for a certainty he did.

"Then you must feed my sheep."

I imagine that the dictate to you and me who want to follow Jesus is similar: Tell others about Jesus' saving grace. Feed those who want to follow Him. Be witnesses to His healing power and His blood on our doorposts.

Invitation to the Feast

A great reward awaits those of us who are willing to follow where Jesus leads. That's the final verse of "Come and Dine."

> Soon the Lamb will take His bride
> To be ever at His side,
> All the host of Heaven will assembled be;
> O 'twill be a glorious sight,
> All the saints in spotless white;
> And with Jesus they will feast eternally.

Yes, my friends. The Bible teaches that a great feast is being prepared in Heaven. Jesus is getting a table spread where we will be fed. And someday that cry will resound: "Come and dine!"

Have you reserved your spot at the table?

There's still room, and there's still time.

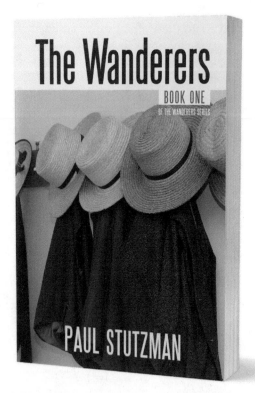

"Young fella, ah knows what Amish is, and you isn't it. Where you frum? Why you runnin' away?"

Leroy L. Jackson, Jr., detected it immediately. Others could see it, too, even if Johnny Miller wouldn't admit it. He was running. Whether he was running from home or toward home, he did not know.

"You're caught in two rip tides," Wandering Willie told him, "but flailing about and fighting it will do you no good. If you fight it, you could die."

"How else do I escape, if not by fighting my way out?" asks Johnny of Willie.

"Wait. Find the edges of the current and make your way back home, wherever that may be."

While Johnny wanders, two Monarch butterflies born on the same Amish farm as Johnny undertake their own long journey, entrusted with the amazing miracle of the fourth generation.

When their journeys collide, Johnny, Sabio, and Mariposa all find that home is much more than they ever imagined.

424 page count · 5.5×8.5" · softcover

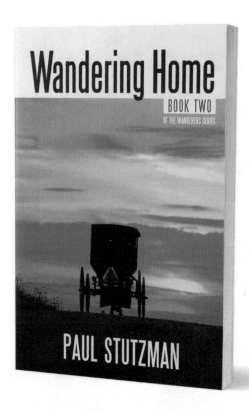

Johnny Miller was twenty-three when he died the first time.

The truck hit him as he pedaled along a Texas road, biking across the country in an attempt to find, somehow, somewhere, a new life.

His old life, you see, had vanished like a vapor.

He thought he had lost everything on the day he lost his dear Annie.

But he will lose far more before finally finding the way that leads to home... and life and peace.

328 page count · 5.5×8.5" · softcover

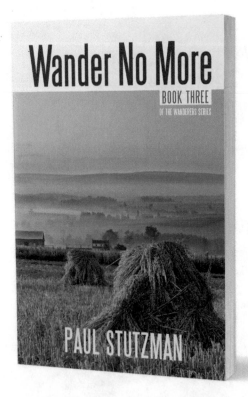

Johnny Miller's wanderings have taken him through tumultuous teen years, growing up in an Amish family; through finding love and then losing his wife, Annie, in a farm accident; and then through the loneliness and agony of a long trek across the United States on a bicycle and on foot. Now he is back home again, farming the land he loves in a quiet Amish community in Ohio.

But although he's not physically wandering, he is still wondering. Wondering why he is restless. Wondering why he feels that some piece of his life is not yet in place. Wondering why, when he was medically "dead," he was met by his wife, who told him his time to enter Heaven had not yet come—he was still needed on earth.

272 page count · 5.5×8.5" · softcover